The real taste of
Indonesia

a culinary journey — 100 unique family recipes

hardie grant books
MELBOURNE · LONDON

'Tamarind in the mountain,
salt in the sea meet in the one pot.'

(Indonesian proverb)

English language edition published in Australia in 2009 by

Hardie Grant Books

85 High Street

Prahran, Victoria 3181, Australia

www.hardiegrant.com.au

Coordination: Claire Eversdijk, Josje Kets, Dunja Schmoll

Art direction & design: Myrthe Bergboer in collaboration with

Kirsti Alink & Suzanne Groenewegen

Photography: Food4Eyes.com, Bart Nijs, Claire Eversdijk, Suzanne Groenewegen

Styling: Lize Boer

Publisher: Pieter Harts

Associate publisher: Mariëm Bellil

Food: Thea Spierings, Marnix van Teeffelen

Printed and bound in China by C&C Offset Printing

Cataloguing-in-Publication data is available from the National Library of Australia.

This book came into being thanks to many people from Indonesia, Europe, Australia and the United States. They made their tried and tested family recipes available to the public. We would particularly like to say thanks to Charles Coors, Geert Claassens, Oma Goudzwaard, Wil van Kol, Peggy Labrijn, Ine de Pruyssenaere de la Woestijne, Robert Sausele, Ilmy van der Ster and Freek Stoltenborgh for their generosity and exceptional inspiration.

Special thanks to Marnix van Teeffelen. With his great knowledge of Indonesian cuisine he has played a vital part in the creation of this book.

This book has also been made possible by Go-Tan B.V.

© Dutch language edition Caplan Books

email: info@caplanbooks.nl

www.caplanbooks.nl

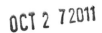

Recipe note: All recipes serve 4 unless otherwise stated.

Contents

Preface

When we started the research for this book on Indonesian (family) cuisine, we had no idea that we would discover such an abundance of culinary material.

It all started with a simple request to the family of one of our editors, whose ancestors originated from Indonesia: 'Would they be prepared to disclose the recipes of delicacies that are always on their table during family celebrations?' They were indeed willing, and this is how we were able to witness the secrets of the irresistible bakmi goreng from Aunt Eef and the delicious traditional *spekkoek* from Opa Coors.

But it did not end there. Word spread like wildfire that we were looking for the best Indonesian family recipes and we learned who we needed to visit for a 'real good *mangoet*', a 'delicious acar (pickle) with cucumber' or who made 'the most fantastic soto ayam (chicken soup)'.

The result was an enormous pile of unique recipes. These were sometimes sent by email, or by post on writing paper or verbally over the phone. And we often received the original family recipe on loan, as it was first written down. It could be scribbled, or carefully written in an elegant script, on almost transparent blue airmail letters, in fragile notebooks with cooking stains and notes in the margin, on coasters or between notes made in camps ... All were equally special, both in the culinary and the historical sense. Incidentally, we also received useful tips, fascinating stories and all sorts of inside information.

After all this, our test kitchen was filled with the most delicious aromas of herbs and spices and the cobek and ulekan – the traditional Indonesian pestle and mortar – became a familiar daily rhythm. During this stage there was still regular contact with the families to ensure everything went as it should. Only then did it occur to us how unique the materials were that we received: an unprecedented variety of pure, honest recipes, with foolproof preparation, and we had the indescribable luxury of working with recipes that have been tested, improved, talked about and experienced through and through, year in year out.

Finally, we combined everything with a solid, general, informative introduction about Indonesian cuisine and its rich traditions and customs to make the book you are holding in your hands. Enjoy the recipes and while preparing them think of the many generations that have prepared these before you.

Selamat makan ...

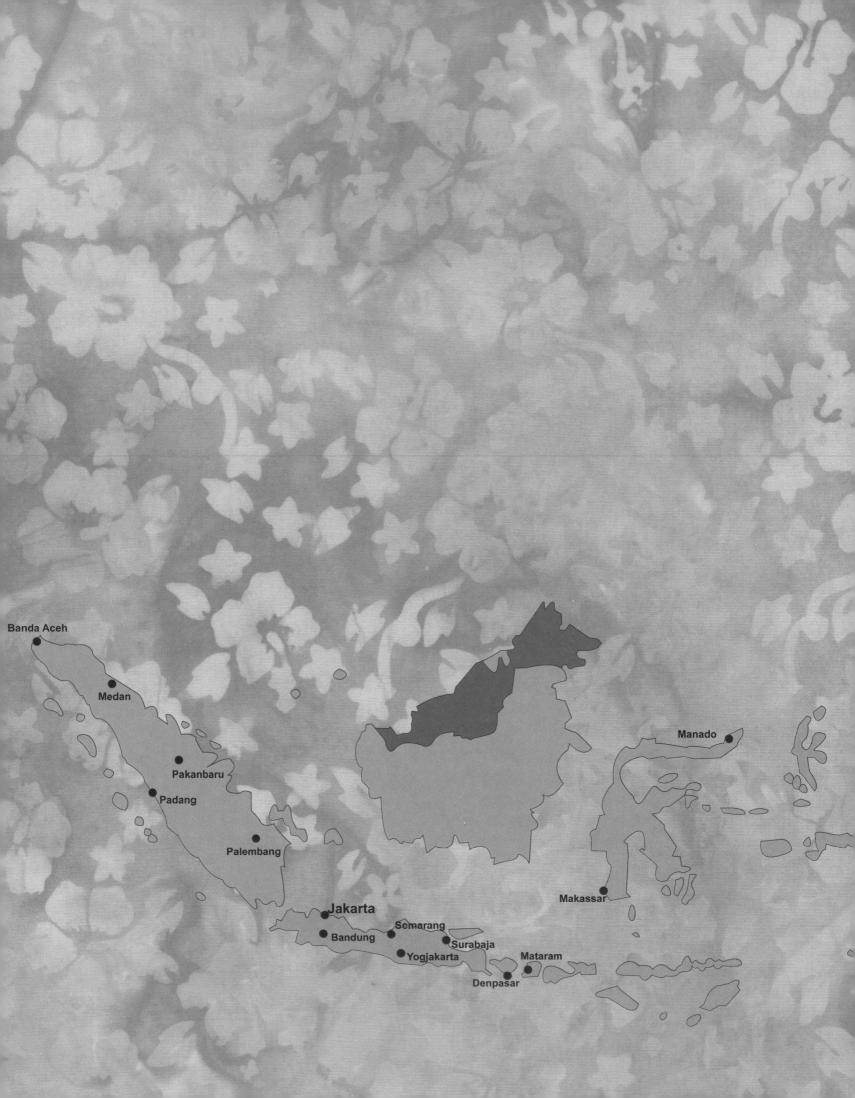

INTRODUCTION

Thousands of heavenly islands together create what must be the most diverse country in the world: Indonesia. Over the course of many centuries, sailors, explorers and merchants from different cultures were attracted by the spices and other riches of the country and left their footprints. Indonesian cuisine reflects this enormous diversity: among others, there are

Culinary folklore

Chinese, Arabian and European elements to be found in the Indonesian food culture.

Many of the more or less isolated island communities still maintained their authenticity regarding preparation, ingredients, specialities and traditions. Even today there are recognisable differences between, for example, the mild sweet dishes from Java and the spicy Sumatran cuisine.

Compared to the rest of the mostly Islamic country, a lot more pork is eaten in Bali, which is influenced by Hinduism. Indonesian cuisine does not really exist: Indonesia possesses an endless variety of cuisines and dishes, all as different and fascinating as the country itself and its surrounding sea.

A kingdom of thousands of islands

The author Multatuli named his beloved Indonesia 'The Emerald Belt'. Those who approach the country from the sea will see an outstretched panorama of lush green islands and smaller islets in the deep blue sea, covered with humid rainforests, dense jungle land and impressive mangrove swamps. Indonesia consists of approximately thirteen thousand islands. Some are the size of a tennis court, whereas others are known as some of the largest islands in the world; with one being practically deserted, while another is very densely populated. The seas and straits which surround the islands are at least as important as the country itself: Indonesians do not just speak of 'our country' but of 'our country and water' (*tanah air kita*). Shipping and trade have always been vital interests and fish still remain a popular food for Indonesians. Further inland you will discover cooler highlands, even glaciers in the central mountainous regions of Papua. Spread over practically all the islands lie hundreds of volcanoes, many of which are still active. These 'fire mountains' (*gunung api*) have left deep layers of fertile ash, rich in minerals, in the soil – so fertile that during the wet months green leaves appear on wooden fencing and cane chairs! Tropical fruit and exotic spices grow in abundance. The east is dry with a savannah climate, high grasslands and scattered trees. The islands Timor and Roti in the southeast have the longest dry period, sometimes for eight months in a row.

Own identity

The 250 million inhabitants of Indonesia are as diverse as the many emerald islands. The country consists of more than three hundred ethnic groups, each with their own identity, their own customs and different appearances. Many of the farming and fishing communities on the islands have lived in relative seclusion for centuries so they now have their own unique food habits. To the original population, the Torajas belong on Sulawesi, the Dayaks in Kalimantan and the Batakkers in Sumatra.

Over the course of many centuries, population groups moved from the Asian mainland to the islands. Later, travellers came from India and China, many of whom settled in Indonesia. From the beginning of the fifteenth century, Arabic merchants and colonists from Portugal, Spain, England and the Netherlands came to Indonesia. For more than three hundred years Indonesia remained a Dutch colony.

'Indonesia must be the most diverse country in the world.'

'The two most well-known Indonesian cooking styles are those from Java, with its mild, sweet vegetable dishes, and the spicy Padang cuisine from Sumatra.'

Chinese influences

Since the thirteenth century Chinese merchants were accompanied on their ships by talented cooks. It was their custom to present delicious dishes to please the sovereigns with whom they wanted to trade. Later, Chinese immigrants came to the Indonesian islands – some with families, but many men married local women and this resulted in a merging of cultures.

Nowadays you find Chinese restaurants and food stalls in every corner of the country. There are hundreds of Indonesian dishes with a Chinese origin, which have been adapted to the local taste, customs and the available ingredients. This is how pork was usually replaced by chicken or beef to make it suitable for the Muslim majority of the population and petai beans ('stink beans', a bean with a very strong taste), chillies and coconut milk were added.

One of the best known Chinese additions to the Indonesian diet – in fact you not can imagine Indonesian food without it – is noodles (mie).

There are hundreds of Indonesian dishes with this originally Chinese staple and nearly every Indonesian town or region has its own noodle specialty – in the capital of Jakarta there are even streets or neighbourhoods with their own noodle dish! For example, the noodles on the island Belitung are served with meat, sliced potato, bean sprouts, cucumber and prawn crackers; mie jawa is prepared in a wok with coconut oil and strips of chicken or beef, spring onion, white cabbage, kecap manis (sweet soy sauce) and trassi (shrimp paste); and the noodles of the Riau island group are prepared with tofu, lettuce, bean sprouts and spicy peanut sauce. The most famous noodle dish is bakmi goreng, fried noodles. There are many variations with all sorts of vegetables, meat, fish or poultry and different herb mixtures. The most important part of its preparation is to cook the noodles for the correct length of time before they are fried, to ensure they remain firm but well cooked.

Indian influences

Since the first century, Indian merchants and Buddhist monks travelled to Indonesia. Their influences are most noticeable in Central Java, where the famous Borobudur temple can be admired, and on Bali, where Buddhism is still an important religion. And so Indian elements have gradually been added over time to the large melting pot that is Indonesian cuisine.

This is how the Indonesian kare directly derives from the Indian curry, even though the herbs used are never identical – the Indonesian versions are adapted to the available ingredients and to local taste. The dish gulai is also derived from Indian curry. There are many types of this dish named after the main ingredient: gulai kambing (curry from goat or lamb), gulai ayam (chicken), gulai udang (prawns), gulai itik (duck), gulai babi (pork) and gulai telur (eggs). It is one of the few Indonesian dishes in which cloves and nutmeg are used following the Indian tradition. Other typical 'curry herbs' that are often found in gulai are coriander seeds (ketumbar), cumin (jinten), cardamom (kapulaga) and cinnamon (kayu manis).

Arabic influences

The influential and sophisticated Arabs have traded with Asia for centuries. In the thirteenth century they brought Islam to Indonesia and this is still the most important religion in the country. The Indonesian language has many words with an Arabic origin. 'Selamat', as in selamat makan (enjoy your meal), selamat datang (welcome) or selamat jalan (have a good journey) are examples of the Arabic 'salam' (literally 'peace'). One of the most noticeable examples of Arabic influences on the food culture is the satay; this method of preparing pieces of meat on skewers was most probably inspired by the kebab. However, the typical marinades and peanut sauce with which satay is served originates from Java. The Indonesian preference for stewed lamb or goat meat is also attributed to Arabic influences.

Wok or 'wajan'

The wok, one of the most indispensable kitchen attributes for those cooking Indonesian food, originally comes from China. In Indonesia, the pan is called 'wajan' and you literally find them on every street corner; in practically every food stall you'll find a wajan above a red hot fire, in which the most delicious dishes are cooked, stir-fried, fried or steamed.

'Spices and roots such as lemongrass, salam, ginger and galangal are simmered in dishes, either whole or in pieces.'

European influences

European colonists also made their mark on the diet of the Indonesian people. The spicy chillies that most Indonesians are so wild about did not originally grow in Asia: they were introduced by the Spanish and Portuguese who brought these with them from other colonies in South America. Now, they simply can't be left out of any Southeast Asian dish. Tomatoes, potatoes, pumpkins and peanuts also came from America via the Europeans. Vegetables such as cabbage, cauliflower and carrots came from Europe and many sorts of sweet pastries are inspired by European dishes. The Indonesian word for cake, 'kue', derives from the Dutch equivalent, 'koek'.

Indonesian and East Indian cuisine

From the blending of the traditions of Indonesians and Dutch people, who colonised the country for more than three hundred years, a separate cuisine originated: the East Indian cuisine. Dutch families who lived in the Dutch East Indies during colonial times learned the local eating habits, which strongly differed from what they were used to, knew and appreciated in The Netherlands. Many Dutch food supplies were not available, or hard to obtain, in the tropics. Their Indonesian *koki* (cooks) taught them some native customs. You still see the mingling of these cultures in the many Dutch-derived words in the modern Indonesian language: for example *buncis* (beans), *ercis* (peas), *panci* (pan) and *semur* (braising).

When many Dutch people returned home after the war they tried to re-create dishes from East India in The Netherlands. Naturally all sorts of new adjustments were made: for example,

the exotic leaf vegetables were replaced by endive and fresh herbs that were not available in The Netherlands were left out or replaced by dried herbs. Often the flavours of hot spices were adjusted to the Dutch palate.

Yet during the past decade it has become easier to obtain many Asian ingredients in Europe. At the same time a growing interest has arisen in authentic flavours and methods of preparation. In Asian food shops and even supermarkets you can now find fresh serai (lemongrass), ginger, chillies and even galangal and kemiri nuts (candlenuts). Because of this, the boundaries between the East Indian and Indonesian cuisine have faded in such a way that it is no surprise that many do not recognise the difference.

(One of the most noticeable Dutch contributions to Indonesian cuisine is the 'rice table'; more about this is on page 32.)

Regional cuisines – Java and Padang

The two most famous Indonesian cuisines or cooking styles are those of Java, with its mild, sweet vegetable dishes, and the spicy Padang cuisine from Sumatra.

People from Java are not originally meat eaters, although you will be able to order lots of different chicken and beef dishes in restaurants. The traditional dishes contain lots of soy products such as tahu (tofu or bean curd), a smooth, silky soy 'cheese', and tempeh, a type of cake made from soft, fermented soy beans mixed with whole soy beans to give it a more solid texture. These nutritious, protein-rich soy cakes are fried in blocks with a mild sambal (chilli paste) and mixed with coconut milk, or wrapped in a banana leaf and steamed to create a dish called botok (which can also be prepared with meat or fish).

Java is also famous for its gula jawa (Javanese palm sugar), which adds a slightly sweet taste to many savoury dishes.

The Padang cuisine from Sumatra uses a lot more meat and chillies. The fiery chilli heat is tempered by a considerable dash of creamy coconut milk but the Sumatran cuisine of the Minangkabau (the original inhabitants) is still known for being very pedas (spicy). Rendang is the most famous Sumatran dish, meant for festive occasions. Beef is slowly stewed in coconut milk until most of the meat has absorbed the coconut oil and is very tender. The Padang cuisine (named after the Sumatran capital, Padang) is also famous for the use of innards: liver, heart, spleen and brains as well as fish heads are served at the table in curry-like sauces.

Babi (pork) from Bali

You can find pork throughout Indonesia at Chinese restaurants and food stalls but the majority of the population are Muslim and therefore do not eat pork. However, on the island Bali about 90 percent of the population are Hindu and you'll find pork in many traditional dishes: for example babi guling (suckling pig on the spit) and babi panggang (roasted pork). A particularly Balinese breakfast or dessert is bubur injin, which is black glutinous rice porridge with coconut and palm sugar syrup. On North Sulawesi pork is also eaten, for example pork satay from Manado, which is not served with peanut sauce but a sweet chilli sauce. With its ever-changing coastline Sulawesi is also known for its fish dishes such as ikan kuah asem, which is a sort of fish soup.

Red, green or yellow Banjar dishes

Popular Banjar dishes come from the largest island Kalimantan and are named after the capital Banjarmasin. Soto banjar is a noodle soup with chicken and garlic. Many banjar meat dishes are eaten with sauces that look red (from red chilli), green (from green chilli) or yellow (from turmeric). You can eat them, for example, in combination with ketupat kandangan (rice steamed in banana leaves).

No rice

On parts of the eastern islands the staple diet is cassava or corn rather than rice. On Ambon the sago palm is the main food source. The pith is removed from the inside of the tree to make sago flour. The pith is crushed and kneaded to release the starch, then drenched with water. The extracted fibrous milk-like residue is strained and dried into starchy blocks. When used in a dish the cook breaks off a piece and heats it in a pan, or roasts it wrapped in a banana leaf above a fire.

The authentic Indonesian dish

The end of the Islamic month of fasting, *Bulan Puasa* (Ramadan), is a major annual event in Indonesia. The majority of Muslims in Indonesia do not eat or drink between sunrise and sunset during this month. When *Lebaran* finally arrives, the big day that announces that fasting has ended, it is time for big family banquets with traditional festive dishes. Buffalo meat in thick coconut milk with serai (lemongrass) and fresh herbs simmers in large pans, and large amounts of chillies and shallots are crushed for sambal goreng ati with livers. Other dishes are full of crispy vegetables, creamy eggs or firm prawns. Festive dishes are spectacular and grand. It is all about the perfect contrast between hot and mild, crispy and soft, salty and sweet.

Not a day without rice

Daily dishes are usually scant for Indonesians – especially in the villages: boiled white rice with some dried fish and chillies. When there are more side dishes, a small amount is mixed with the rice for taste. Certainly meat and fish are not consumed in the amounts we are used to. Therefore, many Westerners experience certain Indonesian dishes as too spicy to eat: they put too much on their plates, while the spicy sauce is meant to be eaten in small amounts with the rice.

Often the women prepare the dinner in the morning and put it on the table where most of it stays till the evening. The main dish will be eaten in the afternoon, but often there are no regular dinner times: the family members can eat from the dishes all day so it is not often that the whole family eats together at the same time. The simple dishes can be eaten warm or at room temperature and heated up again for evening dinner.

The custom of eating at irregular times has moved to the cities: there you can buy simple dishes all day at small local stalls – fresh stir-fried noodles, a well-filled soto (Indonesian soup) with chicken and vegetables, or satay grilled in front of you with pieces of cold sticky rice (lontong) to dip into your peanut sauce. Many people in the cities do not cook for themselves every day but eat the healthy and cheap dishes served in simple food stalls on the streets.

Magnificent party food

Special occasions in Indonesia go hand in hand with lavish dishes. Family celebrations such as a circumcision party, harvest festival or a wedding demand lavish banquets. The women are often busy for days preparing the most delicious dishes. Everyone does their part and, at the same time, they try to outdo each other with the best sayur or sambal. Instead of the usual white rice there is a cone-shaped mountain of nasi kuning placed at the heart of the dish. This fragrant rice is made with pandan and coconut and is the beautiful golden yellow colour of turmeric – the colour of wealth, prosperity and happiness. The end of the fasting month of Ramadan is also exuberantly celebrated by Indonesian Muslims with traditional dishes and sweet rice cookies.

Contrasts

But how do you prepare a beautiful Indonesian dish yourself? A typical meal consists of rice, accompanied by one or two savoury side dishes with vegetables, meat or fish and one or two garnishes such as spicy sambal, serundeng (grated coconut) or emping (crackers). For grander or festive dinners you can choose further side dishes and garnishes and maybe some of these will require more complicated methods of preparation. The most important thing when organising a feast is to select dishes that contrast in texture, flavour and composition. If, for instance, you are serving a sayur, a 'wet' vegetable dish with a spicy, almost soup-like sauce of coconut milk, you should choose a 'dry' dish such as ayam panggang, roasted chicken, to go with it. With thick, creamy sauces such as peanut sauce, something crispy would be delicious; think of crispy fried tahu goreng, fried onions or prawn crackers. A few soft, stewed meat or vegetable dishes require a crisp salad. Make sure that you have a variety of flavours, such as a spicy dish with some fresh pickle acar ketimun and a mild sweet dish with a sauce of kecap manis. As far as the main ingredients are concerned, you can create a lot of variation by choosing, for example, a meat dish, a dish with fish or prawns and one or two dishes with vegetables, tempeh or egg. You must have a sambal of spicy chillies on the table, which each person can put on the side of their plate according to their own taste – or choose two different sambals such as a very hot spicy one and a milder fried one.

'Indonesian cuisine does not really exist: Indonesia possesses an endless variety of cuisines and dishes, all as different and fascinating as the country itself and its surrounding sea.'

Etiquette

When you are a guest at an Indonesian family meal you can be sure that there will be more food on the table than can be eaten – this is a sign of hospitality. In Indonesia they usually eat with spoon (right hand) and fork (left hand) but sometimes only with the right hand (the left hand is seen as unclean). It is customary to wait until the hostess or host invites you to eat with a friendly '*Silakan!*' (something like 'Help yourself!') or simply '*Makan!*' ('Eat!') before you eat. You then dish up some rice into your plate or bowl and, next to this, small amounts of the different side dishes. Remember that the rice is the main part of the meal, so do not fill your plate with meat or fish. You continue eating a little of each side dish with the rice and, when the sauce on your plate is finished, you take some more from the communal dishes on the table. This way of putting small portions on your plate several times also shows that you are enjoying your meal. To emphasise the appreciated hospitality towards the person who invited you, you do not finish your whole plate, and you also leave a drop at the bottom of your glass.

Traditional and modern

In their authentic dishes, most Indonesian families will not discard any of the meat or fish they use. Fish is prepared with bones and meat is still attached to the bone, including gristle and fat. Sauces are usually fairly coarse in texture. Cooks at good Indonesian restaurants often make more modern versions of dishes and you could do this at home too: they use the same authentic herb mixtures, but combine these with fillets of meat or fish. They also strain certain sauces to remove coarse, hard pieces. This does not really affect the flavour and the dishes look more appetising and (according to our standards) are more pleasant to eat.

Too many pans?

An Indonesian festive meal with so many different dishes may cause problems in a Western kitchen if you do not have enough cooking rings for all the pans. Using the oven may be one way to keep dishes warm, especially meat dishes that need slow cooking, such as rendang (which you can simply put into a serving dish, cover with aluminium foil and keep warm in the oven at 100°C/210°F). The same goes for eggs, fish and prawns served in a sauce – just do not keep these dishes warm for more than half an hour or they will become dry. It's usually better to prepare vegetable dishes at the last minute to ensure that the vegetables are not overcooked and maintain their texture.

Enjoying a rice table

The rice table was introduced by Dutch colonists, who were used to eating a lot more meat and fish at home than was customary in Indonesia. During the twenties and thirties in the last century, the 'classic rice table' was served on Sundays in the Hotel des Indes in Batavia (the name given by the Dutch to the capital Jakarta). This Sunday lunch was inspired by the festive dishes ('makan besar', something like 'grand dinner') that were created maybe once or twice a year in Indonesian villages. For the Dutch planters and traders this was a way to demonstrate and celebrate the many riches of the colony. These feasts became bigger and more elaborate: there are tales of rice tables with more than two hundred dishes being served.

Since then the whole world has embraced the idea of the rice table. At its best it is a wonderful medley of flavours and spices and fresh dishes, which accompany steamed white rice. And at its worst, it's an 'all you can eat' buffet of dishes that have been kept warm for too long and have been adapted to Western taste and featuring tourists piling up their plates as high as possible. However, the rice table remains a beautiful way of becoming acquainted with the flavours of Indonesian dishes and of putting special dishes on the table at home. A well-prepared rice table is a real culinary experience! Always make sure that the rice is the main ingredient and that the individual flavours of the dishes are done justice.

In the glass

Usually coffee, tea or water accompanies a dish. Cold fruit juices or tea brewed from slices of ginger root (good for the digestion!) can also be refreshing. Muslims obviously do not consume alcohol but many Westerners love a cold beer with an Indonesian dish or rice table. (Often they drink beer to 'put out the fire' caused by the spicy heat of sambal, although this does not really work; the best remedy for a burning sensation in your mouth is a bite of dry white rice.)

There seems to be a persistent prejudice that Indonesian cuisine does not combine well with wine, however the opposite is true. Aromatic, fruity wines that do not contain a lot of tannin are a perfect companion for the exotic flavours of spices, herbs and coconut. Sweet drinks such as cendol (with coconut and ice) and jus alpokat (a type of avocado milkshake, often with a hint of chocolate) are more suitable as a snack or dessert. These are not consumed during the main course.

'There are tales of rice tables with more than two hundred dishes being served.'

And for dessert ...

Fresh, juicy tropical fruit is a lovely conclusion to any dinner. Sweet pineapples and aromatic mangos, refreshing small lychees and rambutans ... you can never have enough. A beautiful fruit salad also makes a dessert worthy of kings. Other Indonesian desserts are often very aromatic, sweet and sticky, with a wealth of palm sugar and coconut cream. These are actually not only for after the main course but are eaten throughout the day as a snack. Try for instance kue talam, a sort of coconut custard, or klepon, sweet, sticky rice balls with coconut. Every rice table should end with coffee from Sulawesi and pieces of sweet thousand-layer spice cake, with all its colourful layers ...

Basic ingredients of Indonesian cuisine

The heart of Indonesian village life is the *pasar*, the daily market at which women meet each other in the morning and buy their fresh ginger roots, onions and fruit for the dish of that day. They do not usually have refrigerators or freezers so the freshness of the groceries depends on how quickly the merchandise is being sold. Crispy fresh ginger and galangal roots, pandan leaves and coconuts may be difficult to find in Western countries.

These days, however, many products that are indispensable in Indonesian cuisine are readily available at Asian shops or even large supermarkets. Some products can be replaced by others. This chapter may be used as a map for a voyage of discovery through Asian food shops: how do you recognise fresh turmeric, is it better to use dried or preserved ginger and what is the difference between 'cream of coconut' and 'coconut cream'?

Rice and noodles

Beras ketan (glutinous rice)

Beras ketan is white short-grain rice. Due to its high starch content, ketan becomes very sticky and soft when cooked, which makes this very suitable for sweet or savoury rice porridge (bubur). You can first soak the rice in water before you steam it to prevent the glutinous rice becoming so soft that it falls apart.

Beras menir (broken rice)

These very small broken grains of rice are usually a by-product that arises during the processing of the rice. Broken grains are removed during sifting of the rice. These cannot be cooked dry as broken rice grains absorb a lot of liquid and are, therefore, cooked to a porridge or are used in steamed or cooked desserts.

Beras merah and beras hitam (red and black rice)

The colour – red or red-brown for beras merah and dark purple to black for beras hitam – is caused by a pigment in the bran. These special types of rice are used for sweet as well as savoury dishes, although less often than plain white rice. Most Asian food shops sell these varieties. Ketan hitam is black glutinous rice that is often boiled into a thick rice porridge and served with coconut and palm sugar syrup.

Beras putih (white long-grain rice)

Rice is by far the most important staple in Indonesia. It is nearly always white long-grain rice, which is simply cooked or steamed until soft and dry. The Indonesian language has many words for rice: for instance, when the rice is cooked it is called 'nasi'. (Although with 'nasi' we immediately think of nasi goreng – fried rice with herbs, meat and/or vegetables – it is really the general word for cooked rice.) For most Indonesian dishes, plain white rice is the most suitable. Sometimes a fragrant type of rice is used, such as pandan rice or jasmine rice (originally from Thailand). Brown rice (with the brown bran still around the grain) is hardly ever eaten in Indonesia. White rice that is uncooked and well stored can be kept for a long time, even years. Once cooked it is better to eat it within two days. Cool down cooked rice quickly and save it in the refrigerator if you would like to use it later. Heat it well in a steamer or in the microwave.

Bihun (rice vermicelli)

Bihun are very thin rice noodles, rather like vermicelli. Usually they do not need cooking but only soaking in hot water until soft (approximately fifteen minutes unless the packaging says otherwise). Then they can be stir-fried with vegetables and pieces of meat or juicy shellfish (bihun goreng), served with peanut sauce and satay or you can use them in a spicy soup. You can also briefly deep-fry dry noodles to make them light and crisp. The Chinese name is 'mihun'.

Laksa (rice noodles)

Rice noodles, laksa, are made from rice flour and water and are a snow-white colour, whereas wheat noodles (mie) are beige to creamy yellow. The Indonesian laksa are thick, round strings and resemble thick, white spaghetti. If you can't find real laksa try to find Chinese rice noodles. These are available in different thicknesses and are flat or round. Usually rice noodles must be soaked in hot water before you use them in a stir-fry dish or a noodle soup (which is also simply called 'laksa').

Lontong (sticky rice cakes)

Lontong, a traditional Indonesian rice dish, is a cushion of sticky rice that is cooked in a banana leaf for a long time so that the grains stick together. It is cut into slices and served cold with, for example, satay. Instead of the traditional banana leaf, you could use a parcel of aluminium foil or a small linen bag. At an Asian food shop you can find special lontong bags with the raw rice already inside. You cook these for a minimum of an hour, leave them to drain and cool and then cut them into slices of approximately three centimetres.

Mie (noodles/wheat noodles)

'Mie' (or 'mi') is the general Indonesian name for noodles. Usually the type referred to is made from wheat flour and water. The noodles are sold dried as 'nests' or straight stalks. You cook them in the same way as pasta in sufficient boiling water, with salt if you prefer. The cooking time depends on the thickness. Noodles have a shelf life of at least one year in sealed packaging. Once the packaging is opened it is best to keep them in an airtight container in a cool, dark place. Some types of mie contain eggs and have a richer taste but a shorter shelf life.

Parboiled rice

Parboiling means that the newly harvested rice grains are soaked in water, boiled or steamed and then dried. Only then is the bran removed by milling and the rice grain looks white. During parboiling natural vitamins from the bran attach to the grain so that at the end of the process the white rice is more nutritious. The flavour is somewhat nutty. Parboiled rice needs to be boiled longer than 'normal' white rice. Do not confuse it with instant rice – this rice is made by heating or rolling white, brown or parboiled rice, which causes small cracks in the grain. This means that the water penetrates faster and the rice is cooked more quickly.

Su-un (glass noodles)

These beautiful, clear, thin white noodles are used in soups, stir-fries and sometimes in sweet desserts. They have a very smooth texture and a mild taste and can be combined with all sorts of ingredients. Su-un are made from ground mung beans (kacang hijau) and are therefore known as kacang hijau mie. Other names for these are cellophane noodles, bean threads, fen si (China) or soo hoon (Malaysia).

Tepung beras and tepung ketan (rice flour and sticky rice flour)

Rice flour is mainly used for making sweet biscuits and desserts such as klepon (sticky balls of rice) and kue talam (a type of rice pudding), often combined with coconut, gula jawa (palm sugar) and pandan leaves, which give the dish a green colour. You can also use it for making sweet or savoury biscuits (rempeyek) or to thicken a sauce. You can buy it at most Asian food shops and it has a long shelf life.

Fresh herbs and seasonings

Bawang (onion and garlic)

Onion and garlic are very important basic ingredients in Indonesian cuisine. Instead of the usual brown onions that we tend to use, small red onions or shallots are more common (bawang merah). The Indonesian word for garlic is 'bawang putih'. The garlic we buy in our shops has much larger cloves than the type used in Asia. The recipes in this book are based on the larger, Western garlic cloves.

Daun bawang (spring onion)

Daun bawang literally means 'onion leaf', and is a type of spring onion. They are used in bumbu, added as seasonings to minced beef, soups, sayur, fish dishes or cut finely and sprinkled over a dish at the last minute. If necessary you can replace daun bawang with young leeks.

Daun pisang (banana leaf)

Banana leaves are not meant to be eaten but are used for wrapping dishes ready to steam or grill. The leaves give the dish an extra gentle flavour. Often you can buy the leaves fresh or frozen at an Asian food shop. If not, you can use aluminium foil to make the wraps.

Jahe (ginger)

Ginger and other roots play an important part in Indonesian cuisine. The fresh roots are by far the nicest. Before use you need to remove the brown skin by, for example, scraping it off with the back of a knife. Fresh ginger root is best kept in a cool, dry place; the refrigerator is too moist. You can also freeze the roots. Ginger powder is mainly used for sweet dishes. The flavour is very different to fresh ginger.

Jeruk purut (kaffir lime leaf)

These fragrant lime leaves grow on the makrut lime tree and have a coarse texture with a bitter flavour. The leaves give dishes a fresh and spicy tang. Usually they are simmered in a dish and removed at the end; if you would like to eat them, they have to be chopped up into very thin strips with the hard centre vein removed. You can easily freeze jeruk purut leaves and keep them for months. At some Asian food shops they can be bought frozen. These are tastier than dried leaves. Grated lime zest is an excellent substitute.

Kemangi (lemon basil)

Kemangi is a member of the basil family and has a lemon-like flavour. The fresh leaves are used as seasoning in sayurs, meat and fish dishes. It is best to add them at the end of the cooking time otherwise they tend to lose too much of their flavour. The dried form cannot be compared to the fresh one. Our 'regular' basil also has a completely different flavour. If you cannot find fresh kemangi then lemon balm is the best alternative.

Kencur (galangal)

Kencur is a root that is best used in moderation for its distinctive flavour. Sometimes it is called 'bitter root'. Galangal is related to ginger. Before use, peel or scrape the dark skin off the roots and cut them into slices or grate them. Dried powder of kencur roots has a milder flavour. In recipes, two centimetres of a fresh root is equal to half a teaspoon of powder.

Kucai (Asian garlic chives)

Kucai resembles a type of chive, often with a bud at the end of the stalk. It is just like chives, a member of the onion family, but tastes more like garlic. It is mainly used for seasoning Chinese dishes such as soups, or to sprinkle on dishes at the last minute as you would with spring onions.

Kunyit (Turmeric, kunir, yellow root, kurkuma)

Kunyit (turmeric) adds a beautiful golden yellow colour to different dishes such as the famous yellow rice nasi kuning, which no festive event should be without. It is the root of the kunyit plant. These resemble small ginger roots but the soft orange inside immediately stains your fingertips yellow. If you are able to find them fresh, make sure you store them properly: you can keep the roots in the freezer for about three months. Kunyit powder adds the same beautiful yellow colour but the flavour is not as fresh and distinctive. Sometimes you can find it under the Javanese name 'kunir'.

Laos (lengkuas, galangal)

Laos resembles a pink ginger root and is used in the same way as ginger – peel and then cut into slices or grate. The flavour is slightly bitter. Fresh laos roots can normally be found at Asian food shops. You can replace them with dried laos, which is usually sold in slices. You will first have to soak these in warm water and before you serve, remove them from the dish. Furthermore, there is laos powder which has a less distinctive flavour. Lengkuas or laos is also called galangal (or large galangal), which can be confusing as there are several galangal roots such as kencur.

Lombok/cabe (chilli):

Chillies come in different sizes and shapes. Generally, chillies are spicier when they are smaller and riper. Red chillies are usually spicier than (unripe) green chillies. (Pay attention as there are exceptions to the rule!) The most 'heat' is in the seeds and the inner membrane; these are often removed for that reason. The seeds have a somewhat bitter taste so it is sometimes better to add an extra chilli for spice instead of leaving the seeds in. Fresh chillies are best kept in a cool, dry place (for up to one week) – not in the refrigerator as it is too cold and moist.

»

Dried red chillies are more con-centrated and therefore more spicy than fresh ones. Instead of fresh chillies you can use a teaspoon of sambal ulek or possibly cayenne pepper (powder). Chilli powder is not suitable. This is a mixture of cayenne pepper, paprika powder and cumin powder. Unless otherwise stated, when recipes in this book are referring to lomboks it is the red chilli (cabe merah) and not the green chilli (cabe hijau).

Pandan (pandan leaf)

Pandan is the oblong-shaped, fragrant leaf of a palm tree (from the screw pine palm family). The fresh leaves give a spicy sweet flavour as well as a bright green colour, which makes them popular for use in cakes such as thousand-layer spice cake. Often you can find the concentrated pandan paste at an Asian food shop. The best pastes will have no artificial colourings. The fresh leaves are also used to wrap food in before continuing preparation or to cook with savoury dishes or rice and remove afterwards. (By the way, this is not the same as is sold in many Western countries as pandan rice: this is fragrant rice that is also called jasmine rice, or sometimes it is a mix of jasmine rice and plain rice. The fragrance of the rice, which does make you think of a pandan leaf, is natural and not added.)

Rawit (bird's eye chillies)

Rawits resemble small lomboks. They are much hotter than their big 'brothers' but the flavour is similar. Cayenne pepper is made by drying these small, hot chillies and grinding them into a powder.

Salam (salam leaf)

Salam is called the Indonesian bay leaf. In appearance the leaves of both plants are similar and they are often used in the same way: the fresh or dried leaves are cooked together with the dish and removed at the last minute. The taste, however, is completely different. Salam is fresher and has a hint of citrus. Fresh salam obviously has the better flavour, the dried leaves or powder have considerably less aroma. Some Asian food shops sell frozen salam leaves, which are the best option if you cannot find fresh ones.

Serai (lemongrass)

Lemongrass has a delicious uplifting and refreshing citrus fragrance but at the same time it is sophisticated and spicy. The stems are often cooked whole in dishes and later removed. To give them even more flavour it is best to bruise them beforehand by pounding them with a heavy object. Some Indonesian cooks tie a knot in the stem to release the juices. The light coloured inside of the stem is lush enough to add to minced beef or to grind into dishes. Serai lasts well for months when frozen. If you cannot find fresh or frozen serai you can use a piece of lemon or lime peel or serai powder.

Spices

Cengkeh (cloves)

Clove trees grow in abundance in Indonesia but the Indonesians themselves prefer to use them for their sweet tasting clove cigarettes (kretek) than in food. Cengkeh is used in some gulais, stews that are inspired by Indian curries. Usually cloves are mixed and ground with other spices into a paste.

Five-spice

Five-spice powder is a typical Chinese seasoning, although it is also used in Indonesia. The five basic flavours are cinnamon, pepper, fennel seeds, star anise and cloves, although some five-spice types contain ginger or cardamom instead of cloves.

Jinten (cumin)

Jinten are the seeds of a plant of the Umbelliferae family. They are mostly used ground in dishes or as part of a bumbu (spice paste). Once ground, the cumin seeds quickly lose their flavour so it is best to buy whole seeds and grind them yourself. Cumin is sometimes confused with caraway seeds, which look similar and belong to the same family. Caraway, however, has a different, stronger flavour.

Kapulaga (cardamom)

To increase their shelf life, cardamom pods are usually sold whole, but it is all about the spicy seeds inside – the pod itself has hardly any fragrance or flavour. If you grind the pods in a mortar you can easily remove the seeds. They have a spicy and sweet flavour. Green cardamom is the most common but there is also a black variety, which is less sweet and has a light, smoked flavour.

Kelabat (fenugreek)

Dried fenugreek leaves are sometimes used in stews but mainly it is the seeds of fenugreek that are used. They resemble small gold nuggets and have a sweet fragrance and a slightly bitter taste. They must be crushed or ground before use. It is best to keep the seeds, like other spices, in an airtight container in a cool, dark place.

Ketumbar (coriander seeds)

The round seeds of the coriander plant give off most of their mild, fruity or flowery taste when they are ground just before use. Therefore it is best to buy whole seeds and grind them to powder yourself instead of using ready-made ground coriander. Keep the seeds in an airtight container in a dark place.

Merica (pepper)

Long before the introduction of chillies to Indonesia in the sixteenth century, Indonesians were fond of spicy food. The 'heat' originally came particularly from the berries of the pepper plant. Black pepper is made from the unripe berries, which have a light red colour. The berries change from brown to almost black when dried. White peppercorns are produced when the berries are ripe; the black outer covering is removed to reveal the white corn inside. Freshly ground pepper is more aromatic than the ground pepper you buy ready-made.

Pala and kembang pala (nutmeg and mace)

Pala is the dried seed of the inner surface of the nutmeg fruit. The covering that surrounds the seed (the mace or kembang pala) is also used in cooking. As nutmeg is very hard it is usually grated. Kembang pala can also be used whole in soups or stews.

Other seasonings

Asem (tamarind)

Asem is the inner part of the oblong-shaped tamarind fruit, which hang as graceful pods in the high tamarind trees. The fruity, sour flavour makes asem a very popular seasoning – Indonesians use it in many dishes just as we would use lemon juice or vinegar. It is very nice with fish and in the spicy fruit salad rujak. The asem also makes meat more tender and is therefore very suitable for all sorts of meat dishes (for example satay). 'Kitchen tamarind' is the pressed pulp of the fruit, which is sold in slices or blocks. These must be dissolved in water and then strained. Easier to use (and similar in flavour) is asem/tamarind paste or syrup, which can be instantly added to a dish.

Cuka (vinegar)

The vinegar used in Indonesian cuisine is usually clear and transparent and fairly neutral, except of course for the sharp, sour taste. It is made from palm sap or cane. Outside Indonesia cuka is very difficult to find but instead you can use white Chinese rice vinegar or malt vinegar (make sure you do not use a vinegar with a strong taste or added herbs).

Ebi kering (dried prawns)

Ebi are small prawns that are peeled, salted and then dried in the sun or fried. You can add them whole or ground to dishes. Often they are soaked first but they are also sprinkled over dishes at the last minute. Be careful as they do have a very strong taste, which will dominate the dish. You can buy ebi pre-packed at most Asian food shops.

Gula jawa (Javanese palm sugar)

Gula jawa is made from the flower stems of the sugar palm and sometimes from the coconut palm. A sweet sticky sap is released by bruising the stems while they are still attached to the tree. This sap is collected, boiled and poured into bamboo tubes and left to solidify, and then cut into blocks. You can buy gula jawa as blocks or slices but also as powder, sugar grains and as a syrup in a bottle or can. As long as nothing else has been added it does not really matter which form you use. It is also sold as gula merah (red sugar), gula aren, gula bali or, as the Malaysians call it, gula melaka. If necessary, you can replace it with brown sugar but this lacks the typical taste of real gula.

Hoi sin sauce (Chinese 'barbecue sauce')

This traditional Chinese sauce is frequently used in Indonesian cuisine. It is a fragrant, strong-tasting sauce based on soy, garlic, sugar, chilli and vinegar. In spite of the common translation of 'barbecue sauce' it is not specifically used for that purpose in Asia. For example, it can be used as a seasoning for stir-fries, as a dipping sauce or to marinate meat or poultry before frying or roasting. Hoi sin sauce is very popular and is usually easy to find, even in large supermarkets. In the refrigerator it has a shelf life of up to one year.

Ikan teri (dried fish)

Ikan teri is usually made from anchovies or sprats. The small fish are pickled and dried so that they become crisp. Sometimes they are sprinkled over nasi and eaten head and all. They are also eaten as a snack, often mixed with fried peanuts. If desired, you can remove the heads from the larger ikan teri. If you wish to use them in a dish, bear in mind that they can be very salty. If necessary you can rinse them under the tap to reduce their saltiness before use.

Kacang tanah (peanuts)

'Kacang' is the general name for beans; the peanut is not a nut, in spite of what most people believe, but the seed of a leguminous plant. In the supermarket you'll mostly find roasted peanuts (kacang goreng). The flavour of raw peanuts (kacang tanah) is milder and they taste more like beans or peas. You can find them at Asian food shops. The best idea is to roast these peanuts yourself to make, for example, the well-known Indonesian peanut sauce, but 'normal' roasted peanuts are fine too. If you use peanut butter make sure it is unsweetened. Peanut oil (arachis oil) is often used for stir-fries.

»

Tamarind fruit

Petai beans

Kecap (soy sauce)

Soy sauce is produced by a natural fermentation process between soy beans and other grains mixed with water and salt. It can serve as a dipping sauce or table sauce but is also commonly used as a seasoning instead of salt. The most commonly used soy sauce in Indonesian cuisine is kecap manis (sweet soy sauce). This is made by cooking the fermented soy liquid with palm sugar, often with added spices and garlic. The sugar makes it slightly syrup-like. When you see 'kecap' in an Indonesian recipe they will always mean kecap manis. Its salty opponent, kecap asin, is usually slightly thinner but still thicker than the similar dark Chinese soy sauce. If you cannot find kecap asin, then this Chinese sauce is a good substitute. Instead of kecap manis you can simply add some extra (palm) sugar to Chinese soy sauce: approximately one tablespoon of sugar per three tablespoons of soy sauce (or see facing page). Other types of kecap you might find are kecap sedang, a mild sweetened sauce; kecap ikan, a kind of fermented fish sauce; and kecap inggris (English sauce), an Indonesian version of Worcestershire sauce. (For more information about kecap see page 190).

Keluwak ('Asian truffle')

'Asian truffle' is the better known name for the seeds of the kepayang (*Pangium edule*), a mangrove tree. This special flavouring is poisonous when raw but the prussic acid in the seeds can be made safe by cooking the seeds for a long time then rinsing them or by putting them on hot coals. The types you find for sale at Asian food shops have already been detoxified and are ready for consumption. (You can tell this by their dark colour; fresh keluwak is white.) The dried seeds must soak in water for several hours before being crushed.

Kemiri (candlenut)

Kemiri are related to the macadamia nut. Like macadamias, kemiri nuts have a high oil content, even in comparison to other nuts. In many dishes kemiri are added crushed or ground, not only for the flavour but also as it thickens the sauce. They must always be added while cooking or stewing as these raw nuts contain a natural laxative! It is best to keep them in the refrigerator. If you cannot find kemiri you can use macadamias or possibly brazil nuts, almonds or cashew nuts.

Petai ('stink bean')

Because of their distinctive flavour and fragrance, petai beans are normally used in combination with other strong ingredients such as garlic, chillies and trassi. Sometimes you'll find them fresh in the pod and you can then double-shell them like broad beans (remove the beans from the pod and then remove the outer casing from each bean). Usually the beans are already peeled and vacuum packed or canned. The fresh beans are green and when dried they become black. The flavour is so unique that you really cannot compare petai with anything else.

»

Prepare your own kecap manis

Experiment with your favourite spices to your heart's content.

100 g (palm) sugar

3 tablespoons water

250 ml naturally brewed soy sauce (without additives)

Chef's flavouring suggestions:

1 star anise

1 serai (lemongrass) stalk, bruised

1 garlic clove, crushed

1 x 2-3 cm piece of laos root (galangal), sliced

1. Melt the sugar with a little bit of water in a pan with a thick bottom. Leave to simmer for a few minutes. Be careful that the sugar does not burn.
2. Add the other ingredients, bring to the boil and simmer for 15 minutes.
3. Strain the sauce through cheesecloth or a fine sieve. Pour into a sterilised pot or bottle.

Kecap manis will keep in the refrigerator for several months.

Preparing your own fresh santan

Fresh santan or coconut milk tastes deliciously refreshing and creamy and has a delightful coconut fragrance. The use of santan makes all the difference to many dishes. You can make your own santan from grated or dried coconut. The easiest way is in the food processor. Put the clear white flesh of a fresh coconut (or 350 grams (12 oz) of dried coconut) into the food processor or blender, together with half a litre of hot water (just before boiling). Leave the processor running for several minutes and then filter the mixture through cheesecloth or a fine sieve. You can repeat this process with the same coconut mixture and fresh hot water; you will get even thinner santan. If you leave the santan 'from the first pressing' you will get a thick creamy layer on the top. This is the coconut cream. If you do not want to use this separately you can just mix it through the 'milk' again. You can keep fresh coconut milk in the refrigerator for two days.

Petis udang (prawn paste)

Petis udang or just 'petis' is a black paste made from fermented prawns, salt, sugar, flour and water, which is mainly used on Java. It has a molasses-like consistency and colour and gives off a strong fragrance like trassi. Petis is a seasoning that, for instance, gives fish soup an extra 'kick' and it is also used in meat dishes and sometimes in the sauce for rujak salad.

Santan (coconut milk)

Contrary to what most people think, coconut milk is not the juice inside a fresh coconut. That clear and colourless liquid is usually called coconut juice or coconut water. Coconut milk, or santan, is made by mixing the grated flesh of the coconut with hot water, kneading it for a while and then pressing it to release the coconut oil. Usually this process is repeated several times so that the santan that is being made becomes thinner and less concentrated with each 'press'. You can buy santan in cans, cartons or blocks in supermarkets and Asian food shops. Usually canned santan contains seventeen percent fat (both saturated and unsaturated fatty acids). Coconut cream is thicker and more concentrated with a fat percentage of around 24 percent. 'Creamed coconut' or santan in blocks is even more concentrated. If a 'block santan' is mentioned in this book, this will mean blocks of 200 grams (7 oz). You can also make coconut milk from these blocks by dissolving 75 grams (2½ oz) in 100 ml (3½ fl oz) of hot water. To make it even more complicated you sometimes also find 'cream of coconut', which is meant for use in drinks and desserts and is therefore sweetened. For use in Indonesian dishes you need unsweetened coconut milk. (See page 126 for more information about coconut and see opposite for 'Preparing your own fresh santan').

Tauco (bean sauce)

Tauco is a thick, salty sauce made from different types of fermented beans and grains, of which soy beans are the main ingredient. The sauce is delicious in dishes with fish (ikan tauco), prawns (udang tauco) or chicken (ayam tauco). Sometimes it may be as thick as a paste or still contain whole soy beans. The sauce is usually sold under the generic name bean sauce or black bean sauce (fermented soy beans are dark brown to black in colour), in cans or glass jars.

»

'Fresh santan or coconut milk tastes deliciously refreshing and creamy and has a delightful coconut fragrance.'

Trassi (shrimp paste)

Do not be put off by the strong, unpleasant smell of trassi! If the paste is prepared well in a dish, the overwhelming odour will disappear and the trassi will give a full distinctive flavour to the sauce. Without it something would be missing from the authentic Indonesian aroma – trassi and chillies are even called the 'Romeo and Juliet' of Indonesian cuisine. Trassi is made from crushed shrimps and other crustaceans, which are salted, fermented and then dried. The result is a thick paste or block, grey to reddish-brown in colour, which smells slightly of cheese. Before use, raw trassi always has to be fried. There are types for sale that have already been fried: trassi bakar, also known as roasted trassi. Both raw and fried trassi must be kept in the refrigerator well wrapped in cellophane. At some Asian food shops you may find the Malaysian style of trassi, belacan. Possible substitutes for trassi are petis (see page 51), Thai or Chinese fish sauce or even anchovy paste.

Wijen (sesame)

Sesame seeds may sometimes be used in a dish along with beef and soy sauce, inspired by Chinese cuisine. Fragrant sesame oil is also used, for example, in vegetable dishes or sambals. Sesame seeds can be roasted beforehand to release the fragrance. It is best to add sesame oil to dishes at the last minute to make sure that the fragrance and flavour do not evaporate.

Basic kitchen utensils and techniques

How do you learn to prepare Indonesian food properly if you haven't been able to learn the secrets from your grandmother? In this chapter you will be introduced to some of the best kept secrets of Indonesian cooking, such as the secret to perfect but firmly cooked dry rice; the magical spice mixtures (bumbu) with their powerful, uplifting aromas; or the smoked taste and wonderful crisp texture of quickly stir-fried vegetables in the wajan (or wok).

You do not need many special kitchen utensils to be able to serve up a beautiful Indonesian dish. If you would like to cook Indonesian food regularly then a good wajan and a cobek, a type of flat pestle, would be good investments. They make cooking Indonesian food easier and more authentic, not to mention more fun, as grinding the spices for the bumbu is one of the most pleasant kitchen jobs!

The versatile wajan

The wajan is one of the most popular Indonesian kitchen utensils. Crisp stir-fried vegetables with red chillies, crisp fried fish cakes, soft steamed rolls filled with spicy minced beef, tasty soups and even stews ... everything can be prepared in this round pan.

'Wajan' is the Indonesian term for the wok, which is found everywhere in Southeast Asia. Originally the pan came from the Chinese province Kanton, more than two thousand years ago. As fuel was scarce, the residents of Kanton were looking for a way to use the heat of their stoves as efficiently as possible. For this reason this round pan was constructed of thin material that conducted the heat perfectly. The pan could be suspended above a fire so that its bottom and sides were optimally heated. Food could be prepared quickly in the wok on a very hot fire. This appears to have even more advantages as we Westerners are now aware: the food maintains much of its taste, texture and nutrition. Also, you need little oil or fat for stir-frying, which in Indonesia was a very expensive ingredient and is today kept to a minimum for health reasons. So it is no surprise that the wok became so popular throughout the world!

Ear handles or stick handle

In China the two 'ears' on both sides of the wok – which were originally intended for hanging the pan above the fire – have been replaced by a long wooden stick that serves as a handle. The wok is placed on a special stove which has an opening at the top where the pan fits exactly. The Indonesian wajan usually still has the two ear handles even though you can also find this pan with a stick handle. This more recent design makes it easier to stir-fry the ingredients in the pan. Which one you find more practical is a personal preference.

Different materials

Most original wajans were made from thin steel plates. This conducts heat very well and if you use a wajan correctly your dishes will get the authentic, lightly smoked flavour. They are less expensive but also less durable than, for example, a cast iron wok. Cast iron is less suitable for stir-frying as it distributes the heat too slowly and holds it for too long. Also, the heavy weight can be a disadvantage. Woks with a non-stick coating can be more practical but they must not be heated too high.

Wajan ring

To be able to place the round pan firmly onto the cooker, you will need a wajan ring (or wok ring). This is a sturdy metal ring into which the round base of the pan fits and it is definitely recommended. You place it onto the cooker with the wajan on top so that it does not wobble but stays in place. (There are now also wajans designed for electric or induction cookers available, which have a flat base.)

A natural non-stick coating

Wajans made from steel plates must be 'burned in' with oil before use. This creates a natural non-stick coating in the pan, which ensures that the food you prepare in it will not burn as easily and will also get a wonderful, authentic smoked flavour.

To 'burn in' a new wajan you only need to clean it the first time with dishwashing liquid to remove the layer of protective oil. Place it on medium heat and as soon as it is warm, pour in three tablespoons of arachis oil or soy oil (no olive oil as this burns too quickly). Use a piece of paper towel to spread the oil over the whole surface of the pan. Wait for a few minutes and again spread the remaining oil carefully over the surface. Repeat this a few times for twenty minutes until the paper towel remains clean. Due to the heating the steel becomes a darker colour.

The wajan is now ready for use but according to many Indonesian cooks it gradually improves after each use. Often they remember one magical wajan that made everything just that little bit tastier. Pieces of meat and fish seemed to get stuck less to the bottom of that old, almost black wajan and the pan gave the dishes its very own, unique flavour that a new pan could never match …

Magic or no magic, it is very important to never wash the pan with dishwashing liquid again, but only with hot water and a soft brush. This keeps the protective layer intact. Dry it off well and it is even better if you place it on the cooker for a short time to dry it completely. If you do not use the wajan daily then grease it with a very fine layer of vegetable oil to prevent it from rusting.

Other kitchen utensils

Cobek and ulekan ('mortar and pestle')

In an average Indonesian kitchen, the cobek does not sit unused even for one day. With this sturdy stone bowl and the accompanying pestle, spicy chillies are finely crushed for sambal and strong spices and roots for bumbu. You can compare a cobek to a sort of mortar but with a different shape: a cobek is more like a dish than a deep bowl. The ulekan, a sort of pestle, is often curved in shape. The surface of the cobek must be rough and irregular so that even rough ginger roots and serai (lemongrass) can be crushed finely. The Indonesian volcanic rock is ideal for this but any other unpolished stone will do. Before you use it for the first time, you should rinse the cobek well with water and then 'initiate' it by crushing a few cloves of garlic so that the garlic juice can be absorbed by the porous stone. After a few minutes you can scrape the garlic pulp out and rinse it with water and a brush (no soap). Dry it well, and it is ready for use.

Kukusan (steam basket)

Kukusans are steam baskets especially designed to steam rice. They come in various materials. Some kukusans have a cone-shaped basket so they can hang in a deep cooking pot without the base touching the water in the pot. (For this you can also use a special steam pan, see elsewhere on this page.) For steaming in the wajan you need a steam basket with a straight base. You place it in the wajan so that there is enough space in the round base part of the wajan for a layer of water. To steam rice you can place a piece of cheesecloth on the base of the steam basket. In these bamboo baskets you can also steam other dishes, such as fish and bah pao (filled, steamed rolls).

Rice steamer

You want always perfect rice without the effort? Then use an electric rice steamer. This contains a water reservoir with a heating element and a tray on top for the rice. For each cup of rice add one and a half cups of water into the steamer, turn it on and wait. The pan will switch off when the rice is ready and switches on when you need to keep the rice warm. You do not have to worry, and the rice will keep warm for at least an hour (or longer), but then the flavour will reduce slightly. Some appliances have two levels, so you can steam rice and, for example, vegetables at the same time.

Steamers

Steamers are available in all shapes and sizes. Usually it is a pan with a perforated tray inside for the rice. If the perforations are too big, as with pans that are not specifically designed for rice, you can place the rice on a piece of cheesecloth in the tray. Steaming rice ensures beautiful, firm and dry grains.

Sutil ('wok spatula')

A sutil is a type of spatula that is used for stir-frying. The 'scoop' is at a slight angle to the long handle, which makes it easier to stir-fry the ingredients in the hot wajan.

'On Bali, the cobek and ulekan are also fondly referred to as "mother and child".'

Washing rice, or not?

Whether or not to wash rice before cooking is often an issue. Most Indonesian cooks always wash their rice. This is not just done to remove impurities such as dust or the polishing residue that is used for the white grains (although the latter does not really exist in Western countries), but also to rinse excess starch from the grains. This makes the cooked rice lighter and less sticky. It is sometimes claimed that by washing you also rinse off a lot of the vitamins, but the amount this would involve is negligible. Some types of rice from the supermarket have been modified so that washing is not necessary; this is normally indicated on the packaging.

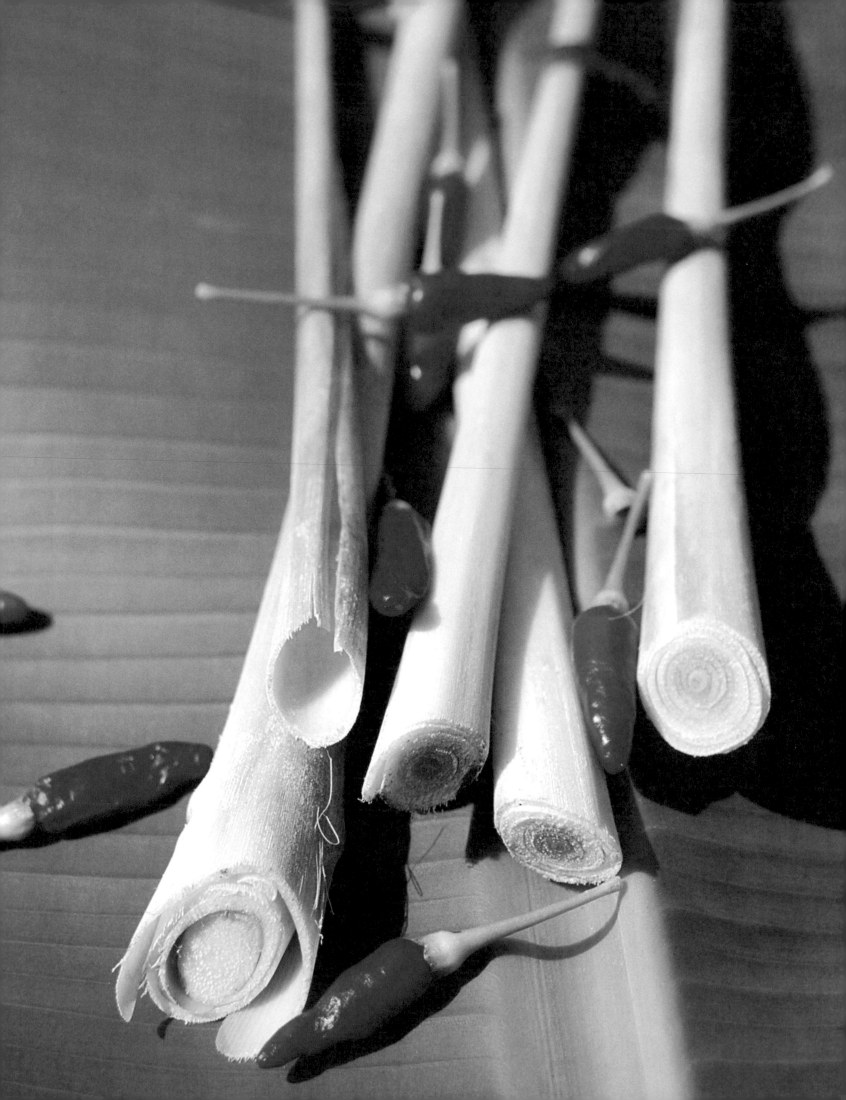

Making bumbu

Fragrant bumbu (spice paste) prepared from fresh ingredients is at the heart of almost every Indonesian dish. Due to the rhythmical bruising and grinding of all the spices, roots and herbs, the flavours are released and mixed into a wonderful smooth paste. The uplifting fragrances which rise from the cobek (mortar) make this one of the most pleasant kitchen jobs.

Prepare all ingredients: hard spices such as coriander seeds are lightly roasted in a dry wajan (wok) to release the oils and to make grinding easier. Peel and clean shallots and garlic and cut hard or fibrous ingredients such as ginger into small pieces. Remove the hard outer stalks from lemongrass and chop the softer inside into pieces.

1.

Spices: firstly add the small, hard ingredients into the cobek, such as peppercorns and jinten (cumin). Grind them finely by making scraping and grinding movements with the ulekan (pestle) — Indonesians do this with a rotating movement from the wrist. When the powder is fine, add the slightly bigger seeds and nuts, for example kemiri (candlenuts), and grind in the same way.

2.

Roots: the peeled and previously cut pieces (or grated) roots are then added to the cobek. Due to their fibrous structure you must apply a little more pressure to grind them finely. At this point of the preparation, stalks such as lemongrass are to be added. Continue until they are finely ground and mixed with the other ingredients.

3.

And the rest: now add the remaining dry ingredients one by one in order of hardness so that you have a beautiful paste. After this you can add any moist ingredients such as vinegar or santan (coconut milk).

4.

Making stock

Many recipes in this book use stock. Here are a few
recipes that are very suitable as a base for Indonesian
dishes. You can easily freeze them into portions so that
you always have some on hand to use for your dishes.

Beef stock

1 tablespoon vegetable oil

2 kg (4 lb 6 oz) beef bones

1 onion, unpeeled, cut into large pieces

4 garlic cloves, crushed

1 carrot, cut into large pieces

2 celery stalks, cut into large pieces

5–10 whole peppercorns

2–3 litres (70–100 fl oz / 8–12 cups) water

1 teaspoon salt

1. Heat the oil in a large saucepan and briefly stir-fry the beef bones.
2. Add the remaining ingredients, except the water and salt, and fry briefly together.
3. Pour enough water into the saucepan to cover all ingredients and stir in the salt.
4. Bring to the boil and remove any foam with a skimmer. Leave to simmer for several hours over a very low heat.
5. Sieve the stock, put it in the refrigerator, then let it cool; there will be a solidified layer of fat on the top that you can remove.

Chicken stock

1 tablespoon vegetable oil

1 whole chicken

1 onion, unpeeled, cut into large pieces

4 garlic cloves, crushed

1 carrot, cut into large pieces

2 celery stalks, cut into large pieces

2 lemongrass stalks, crushed

4 kaffir lime leaves

5–10 whole peppercorns

2–3 litres (70–100 fl oz / 8–12 cups) water

1 teaspoon salt

1. Heat the oil in a large saucepan and briefly fry the chicken.
2. Add the remaining ingredients, except the water and salt, and briefly fry together without browning them.
3. Pour enough water into the saucepan to cover all ingredients and stir in the salt. Bring to the boil and remove the foam with a skimmer. Leave to simmer over a very low heat for 1 hour. Remove the chicken, let it cool then remove the meat from the bones (you can use the meat for another dish).
4. Put the bones back into the saucepan and leave to simmer for another hour.
5. Sieve the stock, put it in the refrigerator, then let it cool; there will be a solidified layer of fat on top that you can remove.

Vegetable stock

1 tablespoon vegetable oil

1 onion, cut into large pieces

2 garlic cloves, crushed

1 carrot, cut into large pieces

3 spring onions, cut into pieces

1 whole tomato

vegetable trimmings from e.g. mushrooms, broccoli, leek, cabbage etc. (optional)

handful of dried shiitake or other dried (Chinese) mushrooms

2 dried red chillies

1 bunch parsley (or only the stalks)

1½–2 litres (50–70 fl oz / 6–8 cups) water

1 teaspoon salt

1. Heat the oil in a large saucepan and fry the vegetables briefly without browning them.
2. Add the remaining ingredients.
3. Bring to the boil and remove the foam with a skimmer. Leave to simmer gently for 1 hour.
4. Pour the stock through a fine sieve and, after it has cooled, store in the refrigerator or freeze

RECIPES

Rice is central to the lives of Indonesians. It is not only the most important basic food but it is also regarded as sacred and therefore has great symbolism in various rituals. Furthermore, rice-growing in the country still decides the rhythm of daily life. Weddings, for example, are held after the harvest period.

Most Indonesians usually eat white rice but there are also delicious dishes prepared with

Rice and noodles

other types of rice. During an important occasion there is almost always a nasi tumpeng (rice cone) of aromatic yellow rice (nasi kuning) on the table. The most important person at the table cuts the tip of the cone and serves this to an older person whom he holds in high regard. But the most well-known Indonesian rice dish is undoubtedly nasi goreng (literally 'fried rice'). In Indonesia this is a typical breakfast or lunch dish to finish leftovers from the previous day. Each family has their own recipe, but the best known variant is served with slices of omelette on top.

Noodles (mie) were (incidentally like fried rice) introduced to Indonesia by the Chinese. Over the centuries, they have become traditional and are often put into soup or fried, either soft or crispy, such as the well-known bakmi goreng (fried noodles).

Nasi Putih
perfect steamed rice

Rice makes or breaks an Indonesian meal. It should be cooked or steamed to perfection: fluffy and soft. Rice cookers are the best way to achieve this, but the following absorption method also gives excellent results.

(long-grain) rice
water

1. Place the rice in a saucepan and add just enough water to cover. Move the grains around with your fingers to separate them. Drain, and repeat once or twice. Drain again and put the rice back into the pan.
2. Add fresh water to the rice; the amount of water depends on the type of rice used. For long-grain rice, use one and a half times its volume in cold water (i.e.: for every cup of rice, use 1½ cups of water). Adding more water results in a softer, slightly stickier rice.
3. Place the rice uncovered over a moderate heat, bring to a simmer, then stir once only with a wooden spoon (any more and it releases starch, making it mushy). Reduce to a very low heat and cook for 10 minutes until the water is absorbed.
4. Cover with a tight-fitting lid that doesn't allow steam to escape (or cover with both a clean tea towel and a tight-fitting lid), turn the heat to its lowest setting – or use a heat diffuser – and simmer for 10 minutes. Do not remove the lid until the time is up. Take the pan off the heat and leave to stand for 5 minutes (the rice will keep perfectly for 10 minutes maximum).
5. When ready to serve, carefully fluff the rice with a fork and transfer to a heated serving platter.

Nasi Kuning
fragrant yellow rice

Nasi kuning is a festive yellow rice dish served at special events. This aromatic rice is usually shaped into a cone called a 'tumpeng'. In Indonesia special cone-shaped rice steamer baskets are available that cook the rice straight into shape. In rural parts of the country however most people use banana leaves folded into a cone shape. While still hot, the rice is spooned into a cone shape, pressed, then turned onto a platter and presented with various side dishes arranged around it.

500 g (1 lb 2 oz / 2½ cups) jasmine rice, rinsed thoroughly until the water runs clear then drained
1 handful glutinous rice (ketan)
3 teaspoons ground turmeric
750 ml (26 fl oz / 3 cups) coconut milk
3 pandan leaves
1 lemongrass stalk, lightly bruised
salt to taste

1. Soak the jasmine and glutinous rice in plenty of water with the turmeric for 1 hour.
2. Drain the rice thoroughly using a colander.
3. Pour the coconut milk into a saucepan, add the rice together with the pandan leaves, lemongrass and salt. Make sure the level of coconut milk is about 2 cm (1 inch) above the rice.
4. Bring slowly to the boil over a medium heat. Reduce the heat and cook for about 15 minutes or until the coconut milk has been absorbed. Stir gently from time to time.
5. Take the saucepan off the heat and leave to stand with the lid on for 10 minutes.
6. Steam the rice for a couple of minutes until tender using a rice steamer – or use a colander placed over a saucepan of simmering water.

Nasi Goreng
fried rice

No cookbook on Indonesian food is complete without a nasi goreng recipe. Use the recipe below as a basic guideline, adjusting ingredients and quantities according to availability and your personal tastes. A well-known favourite of many Indonesians is nasi goreng with ikan jambal (salted dried fish). The fish replaces both meat and prawns and should be cooked for 10 minutes in boiling water before use, then rinsed under the cold tap and cut into small pieces. Regardless of which version of nasi goreng you like best, always serve it with freshly prepared sambal, (home fried) prawn crackers (krupuk) and a refreshing acar (pickled vegetables), for example Acar Ketimun (see page 118).

2 tablespoons vegetable oil
1 small stock cube, crumbled
200 g (7 oz) bacon lardons (or small cubes of pork, chicken or prawns)
1 baby leek or 2 spring onions, thinly sliced
600 g (1lb 5 oz) cold, cooked jasmine rice
3 eggs, beaten with 2 tablespoons milk

For the bumbu:
4 shallots, finely chopped
2 garlic cloves, finely chopped
2 teaspoons Sambal Ulek (page 238) or 2 lomboks (large red chillies), seeded and finely chopped
1 heaped teaspoon trassi bakar (roasted dried shrimp paste), crumbled

1. Pound all bumbu ingredients to a smooth paste using a pestle and mortar.
2. Gently cook the bumbu in 1 tablespoon of oil in a wok until fragrant, for about 3 minutes, then stir in the crumbled stock cube.
3. Tip in the lardons or meat/prawns and stir-fry for approx. 3 minutes. Add the leek or spring onion.
4. Gradually mix in the rice – separate the grains beforehand – and toss gently until everything is piping hot. Turn out onto a warm serving dish.
5. Heat the remaining oil in the wok, add the egg mixture and cook to make an omelette. Cut the omelette into strips and serve on top of the rice.

No salt

In many Asian countries, the worst thing a cook can do is to forget to put salt in the rice. But not in Indonesia: they traditionally cook the rice without salt. The perfect, light, snow-white grains are the pinnacle of purity on the table and do not need any addition. Salt and spices are in the side dishes and you mix small amounts into the white rice when eating.

Lontong
sticky rice cakes

Lontong is sticky rice that is cooked in a pouch and cut into cubes. Pouches containing the raw rice are available from Indonesian food shops. Three pouches will serve at least four people.

3 pouches lontong

1. Boil the pouches of lontong in enough water until the rice is 3–4 times its original volume. This should take around 2 hours.
2. Remove the pouches from the saucepan and allow them to cool completely.
3. Remove the plastic and cut the lontong into cubes.

Tip: Always serve lontong cold, perhaps with Gado-gado (see page 90) or any other vegetable dish. Lontong is delicious when served with Simple Kecap Sauce (see page 199).

Rice legend

Many Indonesians never completely empty their rice pan as this would bring bad luck. This superstition is based on an old legend. One night a young rice farmer, Joko Tarub, was walking near his fields when he saw the goddess Nawang Wulan and her friends bathing in a spring. Bewitched by her beauty he hid her winged robe under the rice in his granary so that she could not fly away. She stayed with him and they had a daughter. As she was a goddess, Nawang Wulan made their meals using only a single grain of rice so that his granary would never empty. She made him promise never to look in the pan. One unfortunate day he could no longer repress his curiosity and he went to the pan and peeked under the lid. Indeed there was but one grain of rice at the bottom. From that moment the spell was broken and Nawang Wulan had to use rice from the granary. As time went by the granary gradually emptied until one day she found her robe on the floor. She put it on and flew back to heaven.

Bakmi Goreng
fried noodles

It's amazing how satisfying eating a bowl of fried noodles and vegetables can be! On top of that, bakmi goreng is a doddle to make and extremely healthy. As with the nasi goreng recipe on page 70, consider this bakmi goreng recipe as a basic guideline and feel fry to experiment with your meat and vegetable combinations. Bean sprouts, prawns or mushrooms can all be added. As long as you keep an eye on the balance of flavours and textures you can't go wrong.

250 g (9 oz) Chinese wheat noodles (not egg noodles)
vegetable oil
4 garlic cloves, crushed
200 g (7 oz) boneless chicken meat, finely chopped
1 small stock cube, crumbled
200 g (7 oz) finely chopped vegetables (e.g. young leek, carrot, celery leaves)
½ pointed cabbage or 1 small Chinese cabbage, finely shredded
salt and white pepper
2 tablespoons kecap asin or Chinese soy sauce

1. Cook the noodles according to the packet instructions. Drain well, then toss with some oil to prevent sticking. Set aside.
2. Heat a little oil in a wok and stir-fry the garlic and chicken for 3 minutes.
3. Add the crumbled stock cube and the chopped vegetables and mix well. Tip in the cabbage and cook, stirring, for a further 2–3 minutes.
4. Toss the noodles through the vegetables using two wooden utensils (wooden forks are good).
5. Turn off the heat and season with salt, a generous amount of white pepper and some kecap asin. Stir once more then serve immediately.

Bakmi Godok
noodle soup

Like bakmi goreng (fried noodles), bakmi godok (literally 'boiled noodles') is originally a Chinese dish. Not surprisingly, in Indonesia you're most likely to find it at Chinese food stalls. It makes a tasty, nutritious lunch.

125 g (4½ oz) Chinese wheat noodles
3 tablespoons vegetable oil
1 onion, cut into half-rings
1 garlic clove, crushed
300 g (10½ oz) lean pork, diced
2 teaspoons ground white pepper
1 litre (32 fl oz / 4 cups) vegetable or chicken stock
1 thin, young leek, trimmed and thinly sliced
handful of celery leaves, chopped
crispy fried onions, to garnish

1. Cook the noodles according to the packet instructions. Drain well, then toss with some oil to prevent sticking. Set aside.
2. Fry the onion and garlic in some oil in a saucepan until the onion is translucent then mix in the meat. Cook briefly, adding the white pepper. Add the stock, bring to the boil then simmer for 5 minutes over a low heat.
3. Mix in the leek and the celery leaves.
4. Divide the noodles into soup bowls and pour over the stock with the meat and vegetables. Garnish with crispy fried onions.

Tip: Thin strips of omelette make another delicious garnish for this bakmi soup.

Gifts from the rice goddess

Most Indonesians eat cooked white rice three times a day. You can recognise how important this basic food is when you see the large number of different words the Indonesian language has for what we simply call 'rice'.

On many of the Indonesian islands you can still find the traditional green rice fields, sometimes on beautiful mountain terraces along the side of a hill, flanked by coconut palms. These rice fields, or *sawas*, demand intensive work. They are constantly under water, which is held in by means of small dams that border the fields; this complex system requires a lot of water. The young rice plants, or *padi*, are planted by hand in the soil. They grow until the rice is ripe and then – often by hand – they are harvested. Of course there is modernisation: harvesters that cut the rice stalks, more efficient irrigation methods, new types of rice … in some places low-flying planes spread rice seeds onto the fields. But a large part of the population is still dependent on the traditional labour-intensive method of sowing and harvesting. For the harvested rice, Indonesians use another name: '*gabah*'. This is threshed and dried in the sun or with hot air. The silver outer layers are buffed off the grains, which are polished until they are snow-white and shiny. The result is 'beras', or uncooked white rice. The grains that are broken during the process are sieved and removed. (This beras menir (broken rice) goes into sweet rice pudding.) Finally, the beras is boiled or steamed until it is totally soft, almost dry and a little bit sticky. This is how Indonesians prefer to eat their rice, with garnishes such as sambal. The cooked grains that appear on the table already have a new name: 'nasi'.

Vegetables

Indonesia has an enormous wealth of different vegetables. In addition to all indigenous species they grow cabbages, soy beans and radishes of Chinese origin. From India came onions, cucumbers, and white, green and purple eggplants. Tomatoes, carrots, lettuces and cauliflowers reached the country via the Dutch settlers. On the daily menu today are many leafy vegetables such as kangkung (water spinach) and other marsh plants, like the leaves of the papaya, cassava and even the pepper plant. Many dishes are a mix of different nutritious leaves, fruit and tubers, such as Indonesia's well-known dish gado-gado. The composition of gado-gado varies greatly from region to region, per season and per cook, but the briefly cooked, crispy vegetables are always covered with a spicy, not too thick sauce of peanuts and coconut.

Kentang Balado
sweet chilli fried potato bites

These moreish potato bites are often served as a garnish or side dish in case a meal needs some added crunch. They also make a very tasty snack or canapé.

2 tablespoons vegetable oil

500 g (1 lb 2 oz) waxy potatoes, cooked until just tender, peeled and cut into bite-sized pieces

1 small stock cube, crumbled

1 tablespoon gula jawa (palm sugar), crushed

a little water (optional)

3 tablespoons (rice) vinegar

For the bumbu:

3 lomboks (large red chillies), seeded and finely chopped

3 garlic cloves, finely chopped

1 large onion, coarsely chopped

1 teaspoon trassi (dried shrimp paste)

1. Pound all the bumbu ingredients to a smooth paste using a pestle and mortar.
2. Heat the oil in a wok and fry the potatoes until golden brown on all sides. Remove from the wok and set aside.
3. Return the wok to the heat, add a splash more oil and cook the bumbu paste gently until fragrant, for about 2 minutes.
4. Add the crumbled stock cube, palm sugar and, if necessary, a few tablespoons of water and simmer for about 2 minutes.
5. Tip in the vinegar and potatoes and cook, stirring all the time, until the liquid has evaporated and the potatoes are crisp.

Gado-gado Jakarta
vegetable salad with peanut and coconut dressing

There are countless variations on this Indonesian classic. This recipe is a delicious version using tofu and tempeh served with a creamy peanut and coconut sauce, garnished with crispy fried onions from Jakarta. Gado-gado tastes best when freshly prepared shortly before serving so the vegetables are still tepid and crunchy.

750 g (1 lb 10 oz) mixed vegetables (e.g. bean sprouts, Chinese or Savoy cabbage and snake beans), cut into bite-sized pieces
3 large waxy potatoes, peeled
4 eggs
vegetable oil for frying
100 g (3½ oz) tempeh, cut into thin strips
100 g (3½ oz) tofu, cut into thin strips
crispy fried onions, to garnish

For the peanut and coconut dressing:
2 lomboks (large red chillies), seeded and finely chopped
½ teaspoon trassi (dried shrimp paste)
½ teaspoon salt
2 tablespoons vegetable oil
50 g (1¾ oz) creamed coconut + 300 ml (10 fl oz / 1¼ cup) water (or use a can of coconut milk)
1 teaspoon tamarind puree
3 tablespoons crunchy peanut butter

1. Cook or blanch the vegetables and potatoes in batches (hard varieties first) until just tender. Drain and set aside. Cut the potatoes into thin slices.
2. Hard-boil the eggs (for approx. 8 minutes), peel and quarter.
3. Heat a layer of vegetable oil in a frying pan and fry the tempeh and tofu in batches until golden. Drain on paper towel.
4. Arrange the potatoes, vegetables, eggs, tempeh and tofu on a platter.
5. For the dressing, fry the lombok, trassi and salt in the oil until fragrant. Add the creamed coconut and water to the pan and stir to dissolve (or pour in the coconut milk). Stir in the tamarind puree and the peanut butter and continue to cook and stir until the dressing has thickened to your liking. Add more water if it becomes too thick.
6. Garnish the vegetables with crispy fried onions and serve tepid or at room temperature with the dressing alongside or spooned over.

Gado-gado
mixed vegetables with hot peanut sauce

Throughout Indonesia you'll find gado-gado at numerous food stalls. Often the vegetables are cooked while you wait, then topped with spicy peanut sauce, krupuk (prawn crackers) or emping (melinjo nut crackers), hard-boiled eggs and deep-fried tofu. Gado-gado is very easy to make for lunch or supper. Feel free to experiment with the vegetables you include.

750 g (1lb 10 oz) mixed vegetables (e.g. green beans, white cabbage, bean sprouts), cut into bite-sized pieces
3 large waxy potatoes, peeled
4 eggs
krupuk (prawn crackers) and crispy fried onions, to garnish

For the peanut sauce:
250 ml (9 fl oz / 1 cup) chicken stock
5 small dried chillies
5 tablespoons crunchy peanut butter
1½ tablespoons gula jawa (palm sugar), crushed
1 tablespoon rice vinegar

1. Cook or blanch the vegetables and potatoes in batches (hard varieties first) until just tender. Drain and set aside. Cut the potatoes into thin slices.

2. Hard-boil the eggs (for approx. 8 minutes), peel and quarter.

3. Arrange the vegetables, potatoes and eggs on a platter.

4. For the sauce, pour the stock into a saucepan, add the chillies and bring to the boil. Reduce the heat and gradually stir in the peanut butter. Continue to cook and stir until the sauce has thickened.

5. Mix in the palm sugar and the vinegar and stir until the sugar has dissolved. Taste and season with more palm sugar and vinegar if necessary.

6. Spoon the sauce over the vegetables and serve tepid, garnished with krupuk and crispy fried onions.

Lalap Ketimun
cucumber salad

This is definitely a salad that should be prepared a few hours before serving. This will allow the flavours to develop and the cucumber to soften without loosing its crunch.

1 cucumber, peeled, halved lengthwise, seeded and thinly sliced

For the dressing:
1 lombok (large red chilli), seeded and finely chopped
1 shallot, finely chopped
salt to taste
1 tablespoon crunchy peanut butter
1 tablespoon rice vinegar
1 tablespoon sugar

1. For the dressing, pound the lombok, shallot and a little salt into a paste using a pestle and mortar.
2. Transfer to a bowl, add the remaining dressing ingredients and mix well.
3. Spoon the dressing over the cucumber, turning to coat well. Leave to stand for at least 20 minutes before serving.

Urap
refreshing vegetable salad with coconut

Urap is THE classic refreshing salad of Indonesia. Make sure the vegetables are not cooked through but retain some bite. In the west of Java, the vegetables are usually not blanched or boiled in water but fried in oil. If possible, use freshly grated coconut – you'll taste the difference!

2 tablespoons vegetable oil

2 kaffir lime leaves

3 cm (1 in) piece fresh kencur root (alternatively add ground kencur to the bumbu)

100 g (3½ oz) desiccated coconut (or 250 g / 9 oz freshly grated coconut)

2 teaspoons tamarind puree, dissolved in 100 ml (3½ fl oz / scant ½ cup) warm water

250 g (9 oz) green beans or snake beans, trimmed and cooked until just tender

250 g (9 oz) white or pointed cabbage, shredded and steamed or blanched until just tender

200 g (7 oz) bean sprouts

salt and pepper

For the bumbu:
2 garlic cloves, finely chopped

1 teaspoon trassi bakar (roasted dried shrimp paste)

1 tablespoon gula jawa (palm sugar)

1 teaspoon ground kencur (if not using root above)

salt

1 tablespoon Sambal Ulek (see page 238) or 3 lomboks (large red chillies), seeded and finely chopped

1. Pound all bumbu ingredients to a smooth paste using a pestle and mortar. If using fresh kencur root, do not add any ground kencur.
2. Heat the oil in a wok, add the bumbu paste and fry gently until fragrant. Tip in the kaffir lime leaves, the piece of fresh kencur (if using), and the coconut and cook for about 3 minutes over a medium heat, stirring all the time.
3. Add the tamarind water and the vegetables and toss everything together. Stir for about 3 minutes until almost all liquid has evaporated. Season with salt and pepper.
4. Allow to cool to room temperature before serving.

Sambal Goreng Kering Kentang
hot and sweet matchstick potato fries

'Kentang' means 'potato' and 'kering' means 'dry' – this dish needs to be fried until everything is completely dry. Sambal goreng kering kentang makes a great side dish to accompany 'wet dishes' like sayur (a soupy vegetable stew) or meat and sauce dishes. For some variation use thin strips of tempeh instead of potatoes.

4 large waxy potatoes, peeled and cut into matchsticks
(or a bag of plain matchstick potato chips)
vegetable oil
5 garlic cloves, finely chopped
1 lombok (large red chilli), seeded and finely chopped
1 tablespoon tamarind puree, dissolved in
125 ml (4 fl oz / ½ cup) warm water
1 salam leaf
2 cm (1 in) piece fresh laos root (galangal)
or 1 teaspoon ground laos
pinch of salt
2 tablespoons kecap manis (sweet soy sauce)
2 tablespoons gula jawa (palm sugar), crushed
3 tablespoons crispy fried onions

1. (If you're using a bag of potato chips, skip to step 2.) Pat the potato matchsticks dry with paper towel. Heat the oil and deep-fry the potato sticks in small batches until golden brown and crisp. While cooking, keep moving them around the pan to prevent them from sticking together. Drain on paper towel.

2. Pound the garlic, lombok and, if using, the laos powder (laos root will be used later) to a paste using a pestle and mortar. Heat 2 tablespoons of oil in a wok, add the garlic paste and stir-fry for a few seconds.

3. Strain the tamarind water through a sieve into the wok, then add the salam leaf, laos root (if using), salt, kecap manis and palm sugar. Keep stirring until thick and sticky, then immediately throw in the potato matchsticks and the crispy onions. Mix well then serve.

Tip: These crispy fries can be kept for at least one week in a sealed jar. Allow to cool completely beforehand.

Sambal Goreng Buncis
green beans in coconut sauce

This spicy vegetable dish tastes equally good with runner beans or snake beans. Add the prawns, if using, just before serving to warm through; they'll end up tough if cooked for too long.

2 tablespoons vegetable oil

1 onion, finely chopped

1 teaspoon Sambal Ulek (see page 238)

1 garlic clove, finely chopped

2 cm (1 in) piece fresh laos root (galangal)

1 tablespoon sugar

salt to taste

500 g (1 lb 2 oz) green beans, trimmed

200 ml (7 fl oz / 1 scant cup) chicken stock

50 g (1¾ oz) creamed coconut, crumbled

1 lemongrass stalk, lightly bruised

dash of lemon juice

1 salam leaf

100 g (3½ oz) peeled and cooked prawns (optional)

1. Heat the oil in a wok over a medium heat and gently fry the onion, sambal, garlic, laos, sugar and salt until the onion is softened.
2. Add the green beans, increase the heat and stir-fry for 1½ minutes.
3. Pour in the stock and bring to the boil.
4. Add the creamed coconut, lemongrass, lemon juice and salam leaf. Simmer over a low heat until the beans are tender. When ready to serve, stir in the prawns and quickly heat through.

A lontong bod C. gebakte uitjes, poer meelblaadje
D. sambal uitjes - nagekook- mesterub
E. soto soep
F. sambal, kemiri

koud gebraade eieren, es paar uien, en di
bijna meelboken.

1/16/ kip in stukken snijden, goed boken,
2 kruiden (6 uien, 2 knofl.p., 6 kemiries, 1 ving
koenir, ½ vingerl. gem kerwatel zout, paar
peperkorrels fijnwrijven & meng opbraad i. olie
3 Meng: wat kipperbouillon, het meuged dr
2 uf hole - bij de andere bouillon dag (3) ke
neide overkook m.st. serch (4) Indien:
ontbeend, z vlees in nette stukje snijde.
Anart Schoteltj: gebakte uitje fijnge meng g
Mikein... klaardj: schoteltj, gemeelte laten
eny voor Spdieru ld. Soep. Segete met laur
a bladen, ontdoen, Sambel: 6 ongebraad
kemiries 2 qr. en paar tl. tmebols (aawit
a st. knip heel fijn gemeren.

Koemyodi garug: (1) pannekoekjes v. bloem: 2 kopj. gerif meu
1 theel do, 1 eidoren, 2t kop. roote (2) Vulul: 1 hele t
Knofl. uie (6 a d uitj.), zeu, peper fijn wrijves, a brad
u pandepek neuel; de ramen gasmak erbij, ien
el graude, fijne prei, fijne rebaug, w. kool), ½ p
fijn varkemsvlees / in het meuge brute eerst faarget
de gemeelte in st. gehakte 2 plakke nisova / fiju
Chermicelly + es mei, bouilley (3) fuylerj u
pann, rollen a, rengel kapein bokken (4) fuie

Tumis Kacang Panjang Udang Tauco
snake beans and prawns in soy bean sauce

Tumis is a stir-fry-then-stew dish made with vegetables, in this case kacang panjang (snake beans), with prawns and tauco paste, which is originally Chinese and made from fermented soy beans. If you cannot get hold of tauco, use kecap instead. Should you prefer a vegetarian version of this dish, simply omit the prawns.

2 tablespoons vegetable oil
2 garlic cloves, thinly sliced
4 shallots, thinly sliced
2 cm (1 in) piece fresh ginger root, grated
2 lomboks (large red chillies), seeded and thinly sliced
2 teaspoons tauco (fermented soy bean paste)
500 g (1 lb 2 oz) snake beans, trimmed and cut into 4 cm (2 in) pieces
100 g (3½ oz) raw peeled prawns
200 ml (7 fl oz / 1 scant cup) beef or chicken stock

1. Heat the oil in a wok and gently fry the garlic, shallot, ginger and lombok until softened.
2. Add the tauco and the snake beans and stir-fry for approx. 3 minutes.
3. Stir in the prawns and the stock, bring to the boil, then simmer until the beans are just tender.

Tumis Buncis
green beans with beef in kecap sauce

For a festive variation, strips of beef are added to the classic tumis buncis recipe, which is usually made with fried tofu or with beans only. Try the recipe below also with chicken livers (fry them separately beforehand and add them at the final stage) or prawns (add them raw and peeled at step 2, or cooked just before serving).

3 tablespoons vegetable oil

1 onion, sliced into thin half-moons

1 garlic clove, crushed

1 lombok (large red chilli), seeded and thinly sliced

3 tomatoes, coarsely chopped

150 g (5½ oz) lean beef, sliced into thin strips

2 tablespoons kecap manis (sweet soy sauce)

1 salam leaf

2 cm (1 in) piece fresh laos root (galangal)

500 ml (16 fl oz / 2 cups) beef stock, warmed

500 g (1 lb 2 oz) green beans, trimmed and cut into 3 cm (1½ in) pieces

1. Heat the oil in a wok and fry the onion until softened. Add the garlic and lombok.

2. Stir in the tomatoes and cook until softened, then add the beef.

3. Mix in the kecap manis, salam leaf, laos and stock and simmer until the beef is tender and just cooked through. Add a little extra water if necessary.

4. Throw in the beans – and maybe some more water – then simmer until the beans are just tender.

Sayur Lodeh
coconut milk vegetable stew

An Indonesian kitchen is not complete without a vast bubbling pan of hot sayur lodeh. This lovely, soupy stew of colourful vegetables in a fragrant coconut broth is usually served with white rice and a sambal. Feel free to add other vegetables.

1 litre (32 fl oz / 4 cups) stock
2 salam leaves
2½ cm (1 in) piece fresh laos root (galangal)
4 shallots, finely chopped
2 garlic cloves, finely chopped
2 kemiri (candlenuts), roasted (see tip below), then finely pounded
750 g (1 lb 10 oz) mixed vegetables (e.g. green or snake beans, white cabbage, bamboo shoots and carrots), washed and cut into bite-sized pieces
50 g (1¾ oz) creamed coconut, crumbled
4 petai beans
1 teaspoon trassi (dried shrimp paste)
2 teaspoons ground coriander
1 lombok (large red chilli), seeded and roughly chopped (optional)

1. Bring the stock to the boil in a saucepan with the salam leaves, laos, shallot, garlic and kemiri.
2. Cook the vegetables in the stock. Start with the hard varieties, which take the longest to cook, then gradually add the others so that they are all ready at the same time. Meanwhile, stir in the creamed coconut, petai beans, trassi and coriander.
3. Just before serving, add the lombok (if using).

Tip: Kemiri nuts (candlenuts) add a nutty flavour and act as a thickening agent. By roasting or dry-frying kemiri beforehand, their taste intensifies and they become easier to grind. To roast kemiri, wrap them in foil and place then in the oven at 160°C (310°F / Gas 2) for 10 minutes.

Sayur Asem Ketimun
vegetable stew with tamarind and cucumber

Adding cucumber makes this spicy–sour vegetable stew extra refreshing. It's great as a light lunch on a hot summer day, served with a sambal (sambal trassi for instance) and white rice. In Indonesian cuisine sayur is a so-called 'wet dish'. It matches perfectly with a 'dry dish' like ikan goreng (fried fish).

800 ml (28 fl oz / 3¾ cups) stock or water
2 cm (1 in) piece fresh laos root (galangal)
1 teaspoon ground paprika
1 large onion, finely chopped
3 garlic cloves, finely chopped
2 salam leaves
1 teaspoon trassi (dried shrimp paste)
250 g (9 oz) green beans, trimmed and halved
1 cucumber, thinly sliced
½ pointed or white cabbage, shredded
2 tablespoons tamarind water (dissolve a little tamarind puree in 2 tablespoons warm water)
handful boiled kacang tanah (peanuts)
sugar to taste

1. Bring the stock to the boil in a saucepan and add the laos, paprika, onion, garlic, salam leaves and trassi.
2. Cook the green beans in the stock over a low heat until just over half cooked.
3. Add the cucumber and cook for another minute or two.
4. When the beans are almost tender, stir in the cabbage, tamarind water and kacang tanah, and add sugar to taste. Serve immediately.

Tears in your eyes

Some people are able to bear the heat of chillies better than others, but the more you eat spicy food, the more your tastebuds become used to it. If the sambal is too much for you then there are two ways to sooth your tongue: cool or distract. Ice or cold water (not carbonated, as that only makes the irritation worse) anaesthetises your mouth a little, so you feel less of the sharp burning of the chillies. In addition it helps to eat something that feels rough, such as rice or prawn crackers. This causes the nerves to be 'distracted' by another signal.

Sayur Asem Jawa
sour vegetable 'soup' from Java

This sour, soupy stew is hugely popular in Indonesia and there are countless versions of it. The sour tamarind (asem) is wonderfully refreshing, especially in a tropical climate. Spoon the sayur into a bowl and serve with white rice, sambal and maybe some fried fish alongside.

3 tablespoons vegetable oil

4 shallots, finely chopped

2 garlic cloves, finely chopped

½ teaspoon trassi bakar (roasted dried shrimp paste)

2 kemiri (candlenuts), roasted (see tip on page 106), then finely pounded

2 lomboks (large red chillies), seeded and finely chopped

400 ml (14 fl oz / 1⅔ cups) beef or vegetable stock

1 teaspoon tamarind puree

2 salam leaves

2½ cm (1 in) piece fresh laos root (galangal)

200 g (7 oz) green beans, trimmed and halved

½ white cabbage, shredded

1. Heat the oil in a wok and gently fry the shallot, garlic, trassi and kemiri until softened. Stir in the lombok and stock.

2. Add the tamarind, salam leaves, laos and green beans and simmer for approx. 5 minutes or until the beans are almost tender.

3. Mix in the cabbage, cook for another minute then serve.

Perkedel Jagung
sweet and salty corn fritters

No one can resist these delicious sweet and salty fritters. They are one of the most popular snacks sold in food stalls all over Indonesia. You can either pound the corn kernels to a smooth puree, a coarse mixture or even leave them partially whole. Fancier versions contain more expensive ingredients like crab meat (perkedel jagung kepiting).

1 x 200 g (7 oz) can corn kernels, drained
handful of celery leaves, finely chopped
2 eggs, beaten
2 tablespoons plain flour
vegetable oil for deep-frying

For the bumbu:
1 onion, finely chopped
1 garlic clove, finely chopped
1 teaspoon black peppercorns
½ teaspoon ground coriander
1 small stock cube

1. Crush the corn kernels to a paste using a pestle and mortar. Transfer to a bowl.
2. Pound all the bumbu ingredients to a smooth paste using the pestle and mortar.
3. In a bowl mix the bumbu paste with the corn paste, celery leaves, egg and flour.
4. Heat the oil. Deep-fry spoonfuls of corn mixture until golden. You need to do this in batches. Drain on paper towel.

Pecel
spicy peanut-flavoured vegetable salad

Just like bakmi soup (bakmi godok), pecel is a typical Indonesian street food. It's sold a lot on trains and buses. Pecel should not be confused with gado-gado. Although they are both vegetable dishes with a peanut dressing, the dressing for pecel does not contain coconut milk and is spicier. Leafy vegetables and cabbage are the main ingredients in pecel. Most commonly used is kangkung (water spinach), in combination with firmer, crisp vegetables such as bean sprouts or cucumber.

250 g (9 oz) cabbage (white, green or pointed), shredded
100 g (3½ oz) bean sprouts
1 cucumber, cut into bite-sized pieces

For the peanut dressing:
1 teaspoon tamarind puree dissolved in 250 ml (9 fl oz / 1 cup) hot water
handful of unskinned kacang (peanuts), skinned
1 teaspoon ground kencur
½ small stock cube, crumbled
1 lombok (large red chilli), seeded and finely chopped
1 teaspoon trassi (dried shrimp paste)
½ jar (175 g / 6 oz) crunchy peanut butter
1 tablespoon gula jawa (palm sugar), crushed

1. Blanch the cabbage (for 1–2 minutes), followed by the bean sprouts (for 10 seconds) in boiling water. Drain and rinse in very cold water.
2. Toss the cabbage and bean sprouts with the cucumber and arrange on a serving dish.
3. For the dressing, strain the tamarind water through a sieve into a saucepan and place over low heat.
4. Pound together the peanuts, kencur, crumbled stock cube, lombok and trassi using a pestle and mortar, then stir this mixture into the saucepan.
5. Gradually add the peanut butter and continue to stir until the dressing has thickened. Add palm sugar to taste.
6. Pour the dressing over the vegetables on the serving dish and mix well.

Acar Ketimun
pickled cucumber and shallots

Spicy Indonesian meals need a refreshing acar (sweet and sour pickle) to calm the palate. This simple cucumber acar is perfect with most meals.

2 tablespoons sugar

3 tablespoons tepid water

3 tablespoons rice vinegar

sea salt and freshly ground black pepper to taste

1 cucumber, peeled, seeded and cut into half-moons

2 shallots, thinly sliced into half-moons

1. Dissolve the sugar in the tepid water. Stir in the vinegar and season with salt and pepper.

2. Pour the dressing over the cucumber and shallot, mix well, then cover and leave to stand for a minimum of 2 hours.

Asinan Manis Cibadak
spicy fruit and vegetable salad from Cibadak

Asinan is a dish of pickled vegetables, sometimes in combination with sweet ('manis') fruit and palm sugar. It's eaten a lot in West Java in the city of Cibadak, mostly as a snack or side dish, or even occasionally as dessert.

1 small pointed cabbage, shredded
1 small cucumber, seeded and cut into half-moons
1 green mango (the variety with crispy, sour flesh) or
1 crispy, sour apple, cut into bite-sized pieces
1 pineapple, flesh cut into bite-sized pieces
4 lomboks (large red chillies), seeded and finely chopped
1 tablespoon gula jawa (palm sugar), crushed
3 tablespoons (rice) vinegar
100 ml (3½ oz / scant ½ cup) water
salt to taste

1. Arrange the vegetables and fruit on a serving platter. Sprinkle with the finely chopped lombok or pound the lombok first to a paste using a pestle and mortar, then toss with the vegetables and fruit.
2. Mix the palm sugar with the vinegar, water and salt and pour over the salad. Allow to stand for about 1 hour before serving so the flavours can develop.

Tumis Kangkung
water spinach with chilli, ginger and shallots

Kangkung is a kind of water plant and member of the morning glory family. Common names include 'water spinach' or 'swamp spinach'. It can branch profusely in moist and wet areas, with stems growing to over 22 m (70 feet) long! Water spinach has a pleasingly mild taste. In cooking, both the hollow stems and the slender leaves are used. Like ordinary spinach, kangkung wilts down tremendously when heated. If you can't find water spinach in your local Asian food shop, use regular spinach or watercress, or even a leafy Chinese vegetable like pak choy or bok choy.

4 shallots, thinly sliced

3 tablespoons vegetable oil

3 garlic cloves, finely chopped

1 tablespoon gula jawa (palm sugar), crushed

2 lomboks (large red chillies), seeded and finely chopped

3 cm (1 in) piece fresh laos root (galangal)

3 cm (1 in) piece fresh ginger root

2 salam leaves

500 g (1 lb 2 oz) kangkung (water spinach), stalks and leaves separated, washed, dried and roughly chopped

1 teaspoon tamarind puree

75 ml (3 fl oz / ⅓ cup) stock

1. Fry the shallots gently in the oil until softened. Tip in the garlic, palm sugar and lombok and stir-fry for 2 minutes.

2. Add the laos, ginger, salam leaves and the stalks of the kangkung.

3. Add the tamarind and the stock and simmer for 2 minutes.

4. Stir in the kangkung leaves. Remove from the heat once the leaves start to wilt (this will only take about 30 seconds). Serve immediately.

Acar Kuning
yellow pickle

This is a spicy type of acar (pickle) that's yellow in colour because of the turmeric. Adding some mustard (of the plain and mild variety) might not be totally authentic, but gives it a wonderfully fragrant kick.

1½ tablespoons vegetable oil

1 teaspoon trassi (dried shrimp paste)

3 tablespoons (rice) vinegar

300 ml (10½ fl oz / 1¼ cups) vegetable or chicken stock

3 cm (1 in) piece fresh laos root (galangal)

1 lemongrass stalk, lightly bruised

1 small carrot, diced

100 g (3½ oz) young green beans, trimmed

½ cauliflower, cut into small florets

2 onions, finely chopped

½ cucumber, peeled, seeded and chopped

2 tablespoons sugar

1½ tablespoons mild mustard (optional)

salt and pepper to taste

For the bumbu:

4 kemiri (candlenuts), roasted (see tip on page 106), then finely pounded

2 tablespoons ground turmeric

3 lomboks (large red chillies), seeded and chopped

1½ teaspoons ground ginger

3 garlic cloves, finely chopped

1. Pound all the bumbu ingredients to a paste using a pestle and mortar.

2. Heat the oil in a wok, add the bumbu paste and fry gently until fragrant. Stir in the trassi.

3. Pour in the vinegar and stock and add the laos and lemongrass. Simmer for approx. 2 minutes.

4. Cook the vegetables in the spicy vinegar broth – first the carrot, then the green beans, followed by both the cauliflower and onion, then finally the cucumber so that they are all ready at the same time.

5. Stir in the sugar, mustard (if using), salt and pepper. Reduce over a low heat until most of the liquid has evaporated, but make sure it doesn't become dry.

6. Take off the heat, allow to cool completely, then cover and leave to stand for at least 24 hours before use.

Coconut: the symbol of life and fertility

The coconut palm is not just a tree to Indonesians, and its rich, sweet fruits are not just an ingredient for use in the kitchen. Coconut is essential in many practical ways and forms part of all sorts of symbolism during birth rituals and wedding ceremonies.

Nothing is wasted from the coconut palm in Indonesia, each part is carefully used. The 'milk' that the Indonesians produce from the grated flesh is the basis of numerous dishes, as is shredded, toasted and steamed coconut and the juice from the young fruits. But the coconut palm provides even more: the palm itself provides shade and material for building houses, the tops and leaves are used for plaiting baskets and making utensils, the juice of the flowers is distilled into a spirit (arak) and the coconut oil keeps the skin smooth. It is therefore not surprising that coconut plays a role as a symbol of life and fertility in many rituals.

Balinese wedding ceremonies are decorated with young coconut leaves and flowers and during a type of blessing ritual the bride and groom receive drops of coconut water on their foreheads and in their hands. During the 'seventh month ceremony' for a pregnant woman and her family, the stomach of the woman is massaged with coconut oil. Then, a young coconut is placed on her stomach. If this rolls off with the 'eyes' upwards, it is a sign that she is expecting a son – if the eyes roll downwards then it will be a daughter.

Indonesian cooking is a feast for vegetarians as there is an abundance of vegetable dishes and preparations using soy products such as tofu and tempeh, and with duck or chicken eggs. The art of preparing tofu, the soft, curdled soybean 'cheese' with an almost sponge-like consistency, was taught to the Indonesians by

Tofu, tempeh and egg

the Chinese. Tempeh is an Indonesian creation. For this, the soybeans are fermented and then compressed into a kind of cake, which is even more nutritious than tofu and has a firmer texture and stronger flavour. Both soy products are very rich in protein and are healthy and therefore excellent meat substitutes. Indonesian dishes are mostly non-vegetarian, as usually a small amount of meat or fish has been used, for example, in the form of paste made from dried shrimps (trassi). If you prefer a completely vegetarian dish just leave these ingredients out or you can use a sweet soy sauce (kecap manis) instead of trassi.

Tempeh Goreng Tepung
fried tempeh in batter

100 g (3 ½ oz) self-raising flour, sieved

2 teaspoons cornflour

small dash of tepid water

300 g (10½ oz) tempeh, cut into 3 cm-long
  (1½ in-long) strips

vegetable oil for deep-frying

For the bumbu:

3 garlic cloves, chopped

2 lomboks (large red chillies), seeded and finely chopped

4 kemiri (candlenuts), roasted (see tip on page 106)

1 teaspoon ground turmeric

1 teaspoon ground coriander

1 teaspoon ground ginger

salt and pepper

1. Pound all the bumbu ingredients to a smooth paste using a pestle and mortar.
2. Transfer the bumbu paste into a bowl and stir in both the flours, together with enough tepid water to make a fairly dry batter (add more self-raising flour if necessary).
3. Dip the tempeh into the batter and deep-fry (in batches) in hot oil until golden. Drain on paper towel.

Tempeh Bumbu Rujak
fried tempeh in spicy coconut sauce

300 g (10½ oz) tempeh, cubed

vegetable oil for frying

1 salam leaf

2 cm (1 in) piece fresh laos root (galangal)

1 lemongrass stalk, lightly bruised

400 ml (14 fl oz / 1⅔ cups) coconut milk

1 teaspoon tamarind puree

1 teaspoon gula jawa (palm sugar)

1 tablespoon tomato puree

salt

For the bumbu:

2 garlic cloves, finely chopped

6 shallots, finely chopped

½ teaspoon trassi bakar (roasted dried shrimp paste)

2 kemiri (candlenuts), roasted (see tip on page 106)

2 lomboks (large red chillies), seeded and finely chopped

pinch of salt

1. Pound all the bumbu ingredients to a paste using a pestle and mortar.
2. Fry the tempeh until golden brown in a generous layer of hot oil in a wok. Drain on paper towel.
3. Heat 2 tablespoons of fresh oil in the wok, add the bumbu paste and fry gently until fragrant, for about 1½ minutes.
4. Add the fried tempeh along with the salam leaf, laos and lemongrass and cook for another 2 minutes.
5. Add the coconut milk, the tamarind puree and the palm sugar and slowly bring to the boil, stirring all the time.
6. Reduce the heat and stir in the tomato puree and add salt to taste. Simmer over a very low heat for approx. 45 minutes or until the sauce has completely thickened. Serve with plain rice.

Tempeh Goreng Tepung

Serve these crispy tempeh sticks as a side dish or snack. You might try this recipe with different types of flour or even a Japanese tempura batter mix (the latter only needs a dash of water, so no cornflour).

Tempeh Bumbu Rujak

The spicy bumbu in this recipe contains dried roasted shrimp paste, candlenuts and tamarind paste. It is originally used in rujak salad – hence its name – but many Indonesians find it so utterly delicious that they also use it in many other dishes. Here it's served with tempeh, but tofu works just as well. Eggs in rujak sauce is another popular dish called telor bumbu rujak.

Tumis Tahu Kecap
fried tofu in chilli and kecap sauce

The soft cubes of tofu absorb all the wonderful flavours of kecap, chillies and spices. If you'd like to replace the tofu with tempeh you can skip the deep-frying in step 1.

vegetable oil for deep-frying

375 g (13 oz) tofu, cut into 2 cm (1 in) cubes and patted dry

2 garlic cloves, finely chopped

2 shallots, finely chopped

2 green lomboks (large chillies), seeded and finely chopped

1 red lombok (large chilli), seeded and finely chopped

1 lemongrass stalk, lightly bruised

2½ cm (1 in) piece fresh laos root (galangal)

1 teaspoon tamarind puree, dissolved in 100 ml (3½ fl oz / scant ½ cup) water

1 tablespoon kecap manis (sweet soy sauce)

1. Heat the oil in a wok and deep-fry the tofu in batches until golden brown. Drain on paper towel and set aside.
2. Pound the garlic, shallot and lombok to a smooth paste using a pestle and mortar. Heat a little fresh oil in the wok and gently fry the lombok paste with the lemongrass and laos until fragrant, for about 2 minutes.
3. Add the fried tofu and the tamarind water and simmer for 5 minutes.
4. Stir in the kecap manis, cook for another 2 minutes then serve immediately.

Ketoprak Tahu Sukabumi
Sukabumi salad with tofu and bean sprouts

This tasty vegetable dish, commonly sold at food stalls in Indonesia, has numerous variations. The version below is very popular in Sukabumi, a city on West Java, about 150 km (93 miles) south of Jakarta. Unlike most versions, Sukabumi's ketoprak tahu doesn't contain peanuts, just kecap, vinegar, sugar and chillies. This gives a deliciously spicy, sweet and sour sauce.

vegetable oil for deep-frying

375 g (13 oz) tofu, cut into 3 cm (1½ in) cubes and patted dry

500 g (1 lb 2 oz) bean sprouts, rinsed twice with boiling water then drained

crispy fried onions, to garnish

For the dressing:

3 garlic cloves, coarsely chopped

3 lomboks (large red chillies), coarsely chopped

1 tablespoon kecap manis (sweet soy sauce)

100 ml (3½ fl oz / scant ½ cup) water

4 tablespoons rice vinegar

3 teaspoons sugar or melted gula jawa (palm sugar)

salt to taste

1. Heat the oil and deep-fry the tofu in batches until golden brown. Drain on paper towel and set aside.
2. For the dressing, pound the garlic and lombok to a paste using a pestle and mortar. Transfer to a saucepan and add the remaining dressing ingredients. Simmer for 5 minutes, stirring all the time. Take off the heat and allow to cool.
3. Arrange the fried tofu and the bean sprouts on a platter, pour over the dressing and garnish with crispy fried onions.

Sambal Goreng Tahu Udang
fried tofu with prawns in spicy sambal sauce

Frying the tofu beforehand makes it firmer and tastier and gives it an attractive golden colour. In Asian food shops you sometimes find ready-fried tofu than can be added straight to the sauce. Don't cook the prawns too long or they become tough.

vegetable oil

175 g (6 oz) tofu, cut into 1 cm (½ in) cubes and patted dry

1 onion, finely chopped

2 garlic cloves, finely chopped

2 lomboks (large red chillies), seeded and finely chopped

2 kaffir lime leaves

3 cm (1½ in) piece fresh laos root (galangal)

2 tablespoons sugar

200 ml coconut milk

150 g (5½ oz) waxy potatoes, peeled and cut into 1 cm (½ in) cubes

salt to taste

1 green capsicum, cut into 1 cm (½ in) cubes

150 g (5½ oz) cooked and peeled prawns

1. Heat the oil and deep-fry the tofu in batches until golden. Drain on paper towel and set aside.
2. Pound the onion, garlic and lombok to a paste using a pestle and mortar. Heat 3 tablespoons of oil in the wok and fry the paste gently until fragrant, for about 2 minutes. Add the kaffir lime leaves, laos, sugar, coconut milk, potato and salt then simmer for 5 minutes.
3. Add the capsicum, prawns and fried tofu, mix carefully and simmer for another minute or until the potatoes are just tender.

Bumbu: the soul of the kitchen

Spicy pastes, or bumbu, form the basis of every Indonesian dish. Every morning in the kitchen you can hear the rhythmic sounds of the pestle and mortar that bring the spices alive and let their delicious aromas fill the air. All ingredients in the bumbu are reputed to have special medicinal properties.

'If rice is the heart of the Indonesian kitchen then bumbu is its soul,' is a common saying. Garlic, peppers, cumin (jinten), coriander seeds (ketumbar) and several ginger-like roots are used everywhere on the Indonesian islands, although the preparation on each island is different. The ingredients are always crushed to a coarse paste in the cobek (mortar). A few minutes of frying in the oil 'opens' the flavours and fills the kitchen, the house or the entire street with exciting aromas.

Mother and child

On Bali, the cobek and ulekan (mortar and pestle) are also fondly referred to as 'mother and child'. They are indispensable in the kitchen. Many people believe that crushing all the different ingredients finely unleashes their spiritual and healing properties, from the uplifting heart-warming qualities of red chillies (lombok) and ginger to the soothing properties of tumeric (kunyit). Nutmeg is good for the digestion, ginger disinfects a sore throat and onion cools the body. Some people even believe that the way in which the bumbu is made affects the flavour of the dish and the body: rapid and powerfully crushed bumbu give energy, while patient, slow, rhythmic movements with the ulekan make the bumbu relaxing and invigorating.

Tahu Pasar
tofu and vegetables with mild kecap sauce

This is a great dish to tuck into after a morning of hard shopping! Literally 'tahu pasar' means 'tofu from the market'. Indonesians eat it as snack, lunch or side dish. Use any vegetables you like.

vegetable oil for deep-frying
375 g (13 oz) block tofu, halved lengthwise and cut into
1 cm (½ in) slices
250 g (9 oz) bean sprouts, rinsed with boiling water then
drained
½ cucumber, diced

For the sauce:
350 ml (11½ fl oz / 1⅓ cups) water
5 tablespoons kecap manis (sweet soy sauce)
1 garlic clove, finely chopped
1 tablespoon sambal brandal*
pinch of white pepper
1 tablespoon crispy fried onions + extra to garnish
2 teaspoons chopped celery leaves + extra to garnish
juice and zest of ¼ lemon
krupuk (prawn crackers), crumbled, to garnish

1. Heat the oil and deep-fry the tofu in batches until golden. Drain on paper towel and cut each slice into 4 batons. Arrange these on a platter.
2. For the sauce, heat the water and the kecap manis in a saucepan and add the garlic, sambal and white pepper.
3. Crumble the onions into the sauce and add the celery leaves.
4. Add the lemon juice and zest to the sauce. Simmer for about 15 minutes.
5. Arrange the bean sprouts and cucumber on top of the tofu and sprinkle with krupuk and extra chopped celery leaves and fried onions. Pour over the sauce and serve.

*Sambal Brandal

Wrap 12 lomboks (large red chillies) and 8 kemiri (candle-nuts) in aluminium foil and roast for 10 minutes in the oven at 160°C (325°F / Gas 2–3). De-seed the lomboks and, using a pestle and mortar, pound the lomboks and kemiri to a paste along with some trassi (dried shrimp paste). Heat 4 tablespoons oil in a wok and cook 2 crushed garlic cloves and 1 finely chopped onion until softened. Add the chilli paste, 2 kaffir lime leaves, lemon juice and salt to taste. Simmer until very soft. Take off the heat and allow to cool completely.

Tempeh Kering
spicy dry-fried tempeh and beef with green chillies

This delicious spicy, dry-fried tempeh and beef with green chillies is the perfect companion to almost any simple Javanese dish. Serve with steamed white rice, slices of cucumber and maybe some stir-fried kangkung (water spinach). Make it suitable for vegetarians by simply leaving out the beef and trassi (dried shrimp paste).

300 g (10½ oz) tempeh
2 tablespoons vegetable oil
200 g (7 oz) extra trim minced beef
4 spring onions, chopped

For the bumbu:
4 green lomboks (large chillies), seeded and finely chopped
1 garlic clove, coarsely chopped
1 small onion, coarsely chopped
1 teaspoon ground coriander
1 kemiri (candlenut), roasted (see tip on page 106)
1 teaspoon trassi (dried shrimp paste)

1. Finely chop the tempeh in a food processor or blender.
2. Pound the bumbu ingredients to a smooth paste using a pestle and mortar.
3. Heat 2 tablespoons of oil in a wok and fry the bumbu paste gently until fragrant. Add the minced beef and stir-fry until loosened. Tip in the tempeh and continue to stir-fry until everything is cooked through and no liquid remains, for about 5 minutes.
4. Scatter with spring onions before serving.

Orak-arik
stir-fried cabbage with scrambled eggs

3 eggs

freshly ground black pepper, salt and nutmeg to taste

2 tablespoons vegetable oil

2 garlic cloves, finely chopped

4 shallots, finely chopped

½ white cabbage (drumhead or pointed), shredded

1 lombok (large red chilli), seeded and chopped (optional)

100 g (3½ oz) ebi (dried shrimps), soaked for 30 minutes in warm water, then thoroughly rinsed and finely chopped

3 tablespoons celery leaves or watercress, to garnish

1. Beat the eggs with a little pepper, salt and nutmeg.
2. Heat the oil and fry the garlic and shallots until softened.
3. Tip in the cabbage and lombok (if using) and stir-fry until the cabbage is tender-crisp.
4. Add the ebi and beaten eggs and continue to stir until the eggs are just cooked.
5. Transfer to a serving dish and scatter with celery leaves or watercress.

Sambal Goreng Telor
curried eggs in spicy tomato sauce

8 eggs

2 tablespoons rice vinegar

3 tablespoons vegetable oil

4 cm (1½ in) piece fresh ginger root

2 salam leaves

2 kaffir lime leaves

2½ cm (1 in) piece fresh laos root (galangal)

3 tablespoons tomato puree

½ tablespoon tamarind puree

1 tablespoon gula jawa (palm sugar), crushed

200 ml (7 fl oz / 1 scant cup) coconut milk

For the bumbu:

4 shallots, finely chopped

3 lomboks (large red chillies), seeded and chopped

2 garlic cloves, finely chopped

1 teaspoon trassi (dried shrimp paste)

½ teaspoon sea salt

1. Pound all the bumbu ingredients to a smooth paste using a pestle and mortar.
2. Cook the eggs in water with 2 tablespoons of rice vinegar until just hard-boiled. Peel once they are cool enough to handle.
3. Heat the oil in a wok and gently fry the bumbu paste until fragrant, for about 1½ minutes. Add the eggs and carefully mix with the paste.
4. Add the remaining ingredients, mix carefully and simmer for 10 minutes over a very low heat.

Orak-arik

Orak-arik means something like 'scrambled' or 'scrambled egg'. You can add all sorts of ingredients to orak-arik, like crab meat (orak-arik kepiting) or tofu and tempeh (orak-arik tempeh tahu).

Sambal Goreng Telor

Hard-boiled eggs are gently cooked in sambal sauce, enabling them to absorb all the flavours and become bright red in colour. You can prick the eggs with a skewer beforehand to allow the sauce to penetrate even deeper into the eggs. Beware not to cook the eggs for too long or the yolks will end up green and dry.

SOTO AJAM.
recept kampschrift Paps,

1 grote kip in stukken snijden. (3 pond soepkip is
genoeg voor c.a. 15 personen)
Bouillon van trekken met een blaadje sereh.
10 sjalotjes
2 knoflookpartjes
8 kemirie (voor de sambal kemirie)
1 vingerlengte koenir(of 2 theelepels gemalen)
1/2 vingerlengte djahe(gember)
zout en peper.
(volgens mams ook 1 theelepel ketoembar en
1 1/2 theelepeldjintan)
kruiden fruiten in olie. Bouillon erbij en doorkoken.
Door een zeef halen en opdienen met
1)nette stukjes ontbeend kippevlees
2)gebakken uitjes
3)fijn gesneden uienloof of jonge prei
4)fijn gesneden selderie
5)in blokjes gesneden hard gekookt ei
6)in blokjes gesneden en gebakken aardappeltjes
   (of frites sticks uit een zakje)
7)mihoen
8)sambal kemirie(een paar kemiries fijn maken, op-
bakken en oelek met trassi en sambal)
9)lontong of rijst
Er kan ook tauge bij gegeven worden.

Opdienen in diepe borden of kommen.
Eerst de rijst opscheppen. Dan mihoen, dan de groen-
ten en daar ruim soep over scheppen.

Chicken

Chicken is a popular ingredient in Indonesian cuisine. Almost every Indonesian family in the countryside keeps chickens, which are usually free range and provide free-range eggs. Most chickens are older when they are slaughtered and therefore the meat is usually boiled first to soften it. This creates a delicious chicken broth, which can be used in many other dishes. Then the meat is taken off the bones and further prepared: either fried or braised. The carcass can go back into the broth to stew a little more until all the flavours are absorbed by the liquid.

Soto Ayam
Classic Javanese-style chicken soup

Soto can be quite simple or elaborate and, consequently, it's eaten both as a quick lunch or as part of a festive family meal. Don't be tempted to replace the su-un (glass) noodles with other noodles. Su-un keep their bite, even after soaking in soup.

1 large chicken (about 1.5 kg / 3 lb 5 oz), jointed
water
1 lemongrass stalk, lightly bruised
4 cm (2 in) piece fresh ginger root
8 cm (3½ in) piece fresh turmeric root (or add ground turmeric to the bumbu)
1 tablespoon vegetable oil
salt and pepper to taste
250 g (9 oz) potatoes
4 eggs
200 g (7 oz) rice (or lontong, see page 74)
100 g (3½ oz) su-un noodles
100 g (3½ oz) bean sprouts, rinsed twice with boiling water then drained
2 spring onions, chopped
chopped celery leaves and crispy fried onions, to garnish
lemon juice (optional)

For the bumbu:
10 shallots, finely chopped
2 garlic cloves, finely chopped
8 kemiri (candlenuts), roasted (see tip on page 106)
1 teaspoon ground coriander
2 teaspoons ground turmeric (if no fresh turmeric is used above)
1½ teaspoons ground cumin
1 tablespoon Sambal Trassi (see page 240)

1. Put the chicken pieces in a large saucepan and add enough water to cover. Add the lemongrass, ginger and, if using, fresh turmeric and bring to the boil. Reduce the heat and simmer for 1½ hours.
2. Meanwhile, pound all bumbu ingredients to a smooth paste using a pestle and mortar.
3. Strain the stock through a fine sieve into a bowl. Take the chicken meat off the bones and tear it into shreds.
4. Gently fry the bumbu in the oil in the saucepan until fragrant. Return the stock and chicken meat to the saucepan, simmer for another hour, then season.
5. Meanwhile, towards the end of the cooking time, cook the potatoes until tender, hard-boil the eggs and cook the rice and noodles. Peel and coarsely chop the cooked potatoes and eggs.
6. In individual soup bowls or plates, layer a small cup of rice (or lontong) and some noodles, bean sprouts, spring onions, potato and egg. Pour over some piping hot broth and some chicken meat. Top with celery leaves and fried onions. Squeeze over some lemon juice if desired.

Tip: This soup tastes great with a Sambal Soto Ayam (see page 246).

Ayam Bumbu Rujak
fried chicken in spicy coconut milk

800 g (1lb 12 oz) small chicken pieces (legs and thighs)
generous dash of white vinegar
vegetable oil for frying
2 salam leaves
1½ cm (1 in) piece of fresh laos root (galangal)
1 lemongrass stalk, lightly bruised
1 teaspoon tamarind puree
1 teaspoon gula jawa (palm sugar)
50 g (1¾ oz) creamed coconut (or small can coconut milk
   + enough water to make up 200 ml/ 7 fl oz/ 1 scant cup)
1 heaped tablespoon tomato puree

For the bumbu rujak:
3 garlic cloves, finely chopped
8 shallots, finely chopped
½ teaspoon trassi bakar (roasted dried shrimp paste)
2 kemiri (candlenuts), roasted (see tip on page 106)
1 tablespoon Sambal Ulek (see page 238, or 2 fresh
   lombok chillies, seeded and finely chopped)
salt to taste

1. Wash the chicken in water with the vinegar.
2. Pound all the bumbu ingredients to a smooth paste using a pestle and mortar.
3. Pat the chicken pieces dry then fry in a generous layer of oil in the wok until golden brown. Remove with a slotted spoon and set aside.
4. Wipe the wok clean and heat 2 tablespoons of fresh oil. Add the bumbu and fry gently until fragrant, for about 1½ minutes.
5. Return the chicken to the wok and add the salam leaves, laos and lemongrass and cook for about 1½ minutes.
6. Stir in the tamarind puree, the palm sugar, half of the creamed coconut (or half of the coconut milk mixed with water), and bring to a simmer.
7. Add the remaining creamed coconut (or coconut milk) and the tomato puree and simmer for about 30–45 minutes or until the chicken nearly falls off the bone and the sauce has thickened. Serve with white rice.

Ayam Bumbu Bali
fried chicken in fragrant Balinese-style sauce

800 g (1lb 12 oz) small chicken pieces (legs and thighs)
vegetable oil for frying
2 salam leaves
3 kaffir lime leaves
1½ cm (½–1 in) piece fresh laos root (galangal)
2 cm (1 in) piece fresh ginger root
300 ml (10½ fl oz / 1¼ cup) water
2 tablespoons kecap manis (sweet soy sauce)
½ teaspoon tamarind puree

For the bumbu bali:
3 garlic cloves, finely chopped
8 shallots, finely chopped
2 lomboks (large red chillies), seeded and finely chopped
½ teaspoon trassi bakar (roasted dried shrimp paste)
4 kemiri (candlenuts), roasted (see tip on page 106)
salt to taste

1. Pound all the bumbu ingredients to a smooth paste using a pestle and mortar.
2. Pat the chicken pieces dry then fry in a generous layer of oil in the wok until golden brown. Drain on paper towel and set aside.
3. Wipe the wok clean and heat 2 tablespoons of fresh oil. Gently fry the bumbu until fragrant, for about 1½ minutes.
4. Return the chicken to the wok and add the salam and kaffir lime leaves, laos and ginger and cook for about 1½ minutes.
5. Stir in the water, kecap manis and tamarind puree and simmer for about 45 minutes or until the chicken nearly falls off the bone. Stir regularly and add more water if it reduces too much. Serve with white rice.

Ayam Bumbu Rujak

Chicken is another favourite to be served with the popular rujak sauce. You can prepare it faster by using breast meat. Simply cook it in the bumbu sauce for 15 minutes or until cooked through.

Ayam Bumbu Bali

Chicken in fragrant Balinese-style sauce is extremely popular throughout Indonesia. If you prefer the bumbu extra fiery, don't be afraid to add more chillies.

Ayam Panggang
roast chicken in barbecue sauce

Ayam panggang tastes best when cooked over a charcoal grill, but an oven also gives an excellent result. The use of typical Chinese ingredients, such as five-spice and hoi sin sauce, reveals its Chinese origin.

1 chicken, jointed (or 1 kg / 2 lb 4 oz chicken pieces
e.g. legs and thighs)
salt
1 tablespoon vegetable oil
2 garlic cloves, finely chopped
¼ teaspoon ground five-spice
1 tablespoon kecap manis (sweet soy sauce)
3 tablespoons hoi sin sauce
100 ml (3½ fl oz / scant ½ cup) water

1. Sprinkle the chicken all over with salt and let it stand for 15 minutes.
2. Heat the oil in a wok, take off the heat and add the garlic, five-spice, kecap manis and hoi sin sauce. Stir well.
3. Mix 1 tablespoon of the hoi sin mixture with 2 tablespoons of water in a bowl and use to coat the chicken. Marinate for about 15 minutes.
4. Preheat the oven to 210°C (400°C / Gas 6–7).
5. Drain the chicken pieces in a colander and transfer to an ovenproof dish. Cook for 10 minutes in the oven, then pour over the remaining water. Cook for another 10 minutes.
6. Spread half the remaining hoi sin mixture over the chicken pieces. Return to the oven and roast for another 5 minutes, turn, then baste with the rest of the mixture. Turn the oven off and leave the chicken to stand for a final 5 minutes before serving.

Ayam Goreng
crispy fried tamarind chicken

It doesn't get much simpler than this: ayam goreng only requires a few ingredients and everybody loves it! Add a little ground turmeric to make ayam goreng kuning (yellow fried chicken).

1 litre (35 fl oz / 4 cups) hot chicken stock (optional)
8 small chicken drumsticks (or other chicken pieces)
2 tablespoons tamarind puree
½ tablespoon salt
250 ml (9 fl oz / 1 scant cup) hot water
vegetable oil for deep-frying

1. Bring the stock to a simmer in a large saucepan, add the drumsticks and cook for about 20 minutes (skip this step if using very small chicken pieces). Drain and set aside.
2. Dissolve the tamarind puree and the salt in the hot water and pour this mixture over the chicken. Leave to marinate for about 2 hours.
3. Pat the drumsticks dry then deep-fry in hot oil until golden and crisp. Drain on paper towel and serve immediately.

Ayam Besengek
fried chicken in fragrant tomato sauce

Besengek can be made with chicken or beef. Made with beef, a big joint is cooked slowly in coconut milk with the spices, then cut into slices before serving. The chicken version is much quicker. In Java, where this dish originates, people sometimes leave the cooked chicken besengek to cool completely in the sauce, then barbecue it later over a charcoal grill, basting it regularly with the sauce.

1 tablespoon ground coriander

½ tablespoon ground cumin

2 teaspoons ground turmeric

5 kemiri (candlenuts), roasted (see tip on page 106), then finely pounded

3 tablespoons vegetable oil

1 onion, sliced

2 garlic cloves, crushed

1 chicken, jointed into small pieces

3 tomatoes, chopped

2 cm (1 in) piece fresh laos root (galangal)

150 ml (5 fl oz / ⅔ cup) tepid water

50 g (1¾ oz) creamed coconut, crumbled

1. Gently dry-fry the coriander, cumin, turmeric and kemiri until fragrant. Take off the heat.
2. Heat the oil in a clean wok and fry the onion and garlic until softened. Add the chicken and tomato and mix well.
3. Once the tomato is completely softened, add the dry-fried spices along with the laos and water. Simmer over a low heat until the chicken meat is nearly falling off the bone. Stir regularly and add more water if it becomes too dry.
4. Just before serving, dissolve the creamed coconut into the sauce.

Sambal Goreng Ati
sweet and spicy fried chicken livers

This is a festive dish of chicken livers cooked in a spicy sauce with a sweet and sour tang. Offal is very popular in Indonesia and there are many delicious ways of preparing it. This tasty recipe might persuade you to put it on the menu more often ...

1 tablespoon vegetable oil

1 salam leaf

500 g (1 lb 2 oz) cleaned chicken livers, chopped into small pieces

100 ml (3½ fl oz / scant ½ cup) strong chicken stock

2 tablespoons sugar

1 tablespoon tamarind puree, dissolved in 100 ml (3½ fl oz / scant ½ cup) water

4 tablespoons coconut milk

1 tablespoon butter

For the bumbu:

1 teaspoon trassi (dried shrimp paste)

2 large garlic cloves, finely chopped

3 shallots, finely chopped

½ teaspoon ground paprika

1 lombok (large red chilli), seeded and finely chopped

1. Pound all the bumbu ingredients to a smooth paste using a pestle and mortar.
2. Gently fry the bumbu paste in the oil until fragrant, for about 2 minutes.
3. Add the salam leaf and the chicken liver and stir-fry for a couple of minutes.
4. Stir in the stock, sugar, tamarind water, coconut milk and butter and simmer until the sauce has thickened and the liver is cooked through. Stir regularly.

Ayam Semur
chicken stewed in sweet soy sauce

This is a mild-tasting curry-style dish, so don't forget to put a tantalising bowl of Sambal Ulek (see page 238) on the table alongside.

1 chicken, jointed (or 1 kg / 2 lb 4 oz small chicken pieces, preferably thighs and legs)
salt and pepper
2 tablespoons lemon juice
vegetable oil for frying
1 onion, finely chopped
3 garlic cloves, finely chopped
2 cm (1 in) piece fresh ginger root
2 tablespoons tomato puree
3 tablespoons kecap manis (sweet soy sauce)
500 ml (17 fl oz / 2 cups) chicken stock
125 g (4½ oz) su-un noodles

1. Sprinkle the chicken with salt, pepper and lemon juice and let it stand for about 15 minutes.
2. Place the chicken in a steamer basket over a wok or pan of simmering water (or use a steamer), cover and steam for about 5 minutes.
3. Heat a generous layer of oil in the cleaned wok, add the chicken and fry until golden brown. Drain on paper towel and set aside.
4. Gently cook the onion, garlic and ginger in 3 tablespoons of oil. Add the remaining ingredients – except the noodles – and simmer over a low heat until the chicken is cooked through, for about 30–50 minutes. Stir regularly.
5. Meanwhile, towards the end of the cooking time, prepare the su-un noodles according to the packet instructions. Drain and serve in a bowl with the chicken semur on top.

Popular spices?

They were literally worth their weight in gold, the nutmeg and cloves of Maluku. The Maluku islands are still nicknamed the 'spice islands'. In Europe, spices were a status symbol: if you could afford them you had to be very rich. Moreover, medicinal properties were attributed to these spices. In order to gain a monopoly in the region the Dutch, British and Portuguese fought bloody wars. Surprisingly, on the islands nutmeg and cloves were never very popular as an ingredient. Indonesians prefer using fresh herbs and roots, such as lemongrass (serai), galangal and salam leaves, and later of course the spicy chillies brought over by the Spanish colonists.

Ayam Paniki
spicy coconut chicken, Sulawesi style

In Sulawesi, where this dish originates from, they used to make it (or maybe still do) with bats, which are called 'paniki'. Thank goodness today the version with chicken (below) is far more popular ...

2 onions or 5 shallots, finely chopped
4 garlic cloves, finely chopped
2 lomboks (large red chillies), seeded and finely chopped
2 tablespoons vegetable oil
1 chicken, jointed (or 1 kg / 2 lb 4 oz) chicken pieces
  (leg and thighs)
1 lemongrass stalk, lightly bruised
2 cm (1 in) piece fresh ginger
2 teaspoons gula jawa (palm sugar), crushed
300 ml (10½ fl oz / 1¼ cup) chicken stock
50 g (1¾ oz) creamed coconut, crumbled
1 teaspoon salt

1. Gently fry the onion or shallots, the garlic and lombok in the oil until softened.
2. Add the chicken and cook until golden brown.
3. Stir in the lemongrass, ginger and palm sugar and continue to stir over a low heat for about 2 minutes.
4. Pour in the stock and creamed coconut and bring to a simmer. Reduce the heat and cook for about 30–50 minutes, or until the chicken is completely cooked through.

Ayam Pedas
fiery hot fried chicken

Only one thing counts here: ayam pedas has to be hot, hot, hot! How hot can you handle it?

1 chicken, jointed into small pieces (or 1 kg / 2 lb 4 oz
  small chicken pieces, e.g. legs and thighs)
vegetable oil
2 onions, finely chopped
4 garlic cloves, finely chopped
4 or more rawits (bird's eye chillies), finely chopped
2 salam leaves
2 cm (1 in) piece fresh laos root (galangal)
2 tablespoons Sambal Ulek (see page 238)
1 teaspoon trassi (dried shrimp paste)
2 teaspoons gula jawa (palm sugar), crushed
½ tablespoon tamarind puree
300 ml (10½ fl oz / 1¼ cup) chicken stock
salt to taste

1. Deep-fry the chicken in batches in hot oil until golden brown. Drain on paper towel and set aside.
2. Gently cook the onions and garlic in 1 tablespoon of oil in a wok. Add the rawit, salam leaves, laos, sambal, trassi and palm sugar and stir-fry for another minute before adding the fried chicken.
3. Add the tamarind puree and the stock and simmer for approx. 30–45 minutes or until the chicken is completely cooked through. Season with salt if necessary.

Ayam Kare Jawa
mild Javanese chicken curry

Most Indonesian curries are very mild, with the exception of gulai kambing. They are thus considered to be everybody's friend.

2 tablespoons vegetable oil
250–300 ml (10½ fl oz / 1¼ cup) chicken stock
50 g (1¾ oz) creamed coconut, crumbled, or 400 ml (14 fl oz / 1⅔ cups) coconut milk
2 salam leaves
2 cm (1 in) piece fresh laos root (galangal)
1 lemongrass stalk, lightly bruised
2 kaffir lime leaves
1 chicken, jointed into small pieces (or 1 kg / 2 lb 4 oz small chicken pieces)
1 teaspoon tamarind puree

For the bumbu:
1 onion, finely chopped
2 garlic cloves, finely chopped
½ teaspoon ground turmeric
1 tablespoon ground coriander
1 teaspoon ground cumin
1 teaspoon trassi (dried shrimp paste)

1. Pound all bumbu ingredients to a smooth paste using a pestle and mortar.
2. Gently fry the bumbu in the oil until fragrant, for about 1–2 minutes.
3. Add a dash of stock and half the creamed coconut (or coconut milk) and bring to the boil.
4. Reduce the heat and stir in the salam leaves, laos, lemongrass and kaffir lime leaves, before adding the chicken and enough stock to just cover. Simmer for approx. 30–50 minutes or until the chicken is completely cooked through.
5. Add the remaining creamed coconut (or coconut milk) and the tamarind puree and cook for a few more minutes before serving.

Tip: Towards the end of the cooking time, add some pre-cooked pieces of potato.

Pastel Tutup
chicken and vegetable pie

'Tutup' means 'closed' or 'shut off' and this pie is covered with a layer of creamy mashed potatoes. The use of mashed potato is adapted from Dutch cuisine, which makes pastel tutup ('*pastei toetoep*' in Dutch) a typical 'Indisch' (of the former Dutch East Indies) dish. Usually pastel tutup is made from leftovers, which means the contents can vary a lot.

6–8 shallots, finely chopped

2 garlic cloves, finely chopped

1 tablespoon vegetable oil

200 g (7 oz) mixed vegetables (e.g. young leeks, carrot and cauliflower), finely chopped

150 g (5½ oz) green beans, trimmed and finely chopped

250 g (9 oz) mushrooms, finely chopped

150 g frozen green peas

2 tablespoons plain flour

1 tablespoon cornflour

dash of milk

salt and pepper

1½ teaspoons freshly grated nutmeg

2 eggs, hard-boiled and sliced

4 tablespoons dried breadcrumbs

For the chicken stock:

1 whole chicken

a small piece of mace

1 young leek, coarsely chopped

1 large carrot, coarsely chopped

2 onions, quartered

2 bay leaves

1 litre (35 fl oz / 4 cups) water

For the mashed potato:

8 large floury potatoes, peeled

100 ml (3½ fl oz / scant ½ cup) milk

1 tablespoon butter

1. Make the mashed potato by cooking the potatoes in boiling water until tender. Drain, add the milk and butter and mash to a puree.

2. Meanwhile, make fresh chicken stock by placing the chicken into a large saucepan with the mace, leek, carrot, onion and bay leaves and pour in enough water to just cover. Simmer for about 1½ hours over a low heat.

3. Strain the stock through a sieve into a bowl, discarding the bones and vegetables. Tear the chicken meat into strips.

4. Gently fry the shallot and garlic in the oil until softened. Add all the chopped vegetables and the mushrooms and stir-fry for 1–2 minutes over a medium heat before adding the chicken meat and 2 tablespoons of stock. Simmer for 3 minutes.

5. Pour in enough stock to not quite cover, then add the peas. Bring to a simmer and cook for about 10 minutes.

6. In a bowl, mix the flour, cornflour and the milk until smooth. Gradually stir this mixture into the casserole and continue to stir until thickened (you may not need all of the flour mixture). Season with salt, pepper and nutmeg, remove from the heat and allow to cool.

7. Preheat the oven to 180°C (355°F / Gas 4).

8. Transfer the cold casserole mixture to a greased oven-proof dish and arrange the slices of egg on top. Cover with a layer of mashed potato, sprinkle with breadcrumbs and cook for about 25 minutes or until golden brown.

Meat

For many Indonesians meat is a luxury restricted to special occasions. Some of the most delicious and special dishes from the Indonesian kitchen originated as a special celebration or even ritual food for a certain event, such as a birth, funeral or a religious feast. For some wedding ceremonies an animal is traditionally slaughtered, and the meat will be prepared later for the bride, groom and guests. Rendang of buffalo or beef belongs to the celebrations of family gatherings and at the end of the fasting month (Bulan Puasa or Ramadan) for Indonesian Muslims.

Perkedel Rempah
crispy fried meatballs with coconut

'Rempah' is the word used for bumbu or spice paste by the Nonya (often spelled as 'Nyonya'), a community of descendants of early Chinese settlers in Indonesia and Malaysia, who, faced with restrictions on the emigration of Chinese women, married locals. The rempah in this recipe is used to spice up the minced meat, which is then rolled into small balls, deep-fried and served as a side dish or snack.

60 g (2¼ oz) desiccated coconut
150 g (5½ oz) minced pork
150 g (5½ oz) minced lean beef
1 teaspoon ground coriander
1 teaspoon garlic powder
1 garlic clove, finely chopped
1 shallot, finely chopped
1 teaspoon ground laos (galangal)
squeeze of lemon juice
2 eggs
salt and pepper
vegetable oil for deep-frying

1. Mix all ingredients, except the oil, and shape into small meatballs.
2. Heat the oil and deep-fry the meatballs in batches until golden brown. Drain on paper towel. Serve as a side dish or snack.

Babi Kecap
sticky pork in sweet soy sauce

This succulent sweet-soy marinated pork dish is commonly prepared for special events in Bali. Marinating the meat several hours beforehand in kecap manis makes the flavour even more intense.

1 onion, finely chopped
1 garlic clove, finely chopped
3 tablespoons vegetable oil
500 g (1 lb 2 oz) boneless pork, either lean or fattier, cut into 3 cm (1½ in) cubes
5 tablespoons kecap manis (sweet soy sauce)
1 tablespoon (rice) vinegar
2 cm (1 in) piece fresh ginger root
200 ml (7 fl oz / 1 scant cup) beef stock

1. Pound the onion and garlic to a paste using a pestle and mortar. Heat the oil in a wok and gently fry the onion paste until softened, for about 2 minutes.
2. Add the meat and cook until browned.
3. Stir in the kecap manis, vinegar and ginger and pour in the stock. Simmer over a medium heat for about 1 hour or until the meat is done. Stir regularly and add a little more water or stock if it becomes too dry. The meat should be very sticky with only a small amount of sauce remaining.

Brongkos
stewed beef in spicy tomato sauce

Kluwak nuts give this dish its intense dark brown colour. The sauce shouldn't be too thick. Brongkos is similar to the East-Javanese dish rawan but with added coconut milk. It can be prepared with different main ingredients, but most often it's made with beef or meat in combination with green beans (buncis) or labu (a type of squash). Occasionally, you'll find it with chicken (brongkos ayam).

3 tablespoons vegetable oil
1 onion, cut into half-rings
3 tomatoes, chopped
250 ml (9 fl oz / 1 cup) beef stock
1 salam leaf
3 cm (1¼ in) piece fresh kencur root (or add kencur powder to the bumbu)
1 slice fresh laos root (galangal)
500 g (1lb 2 oz) boneless stewing beef, cubed
salt (optional)
50 g (1¾ oz) creamed coconut, grated
1–2 teaspoons sugar
6 eggs, hard-boiled, peeled and halved

For the bumbu:
5 kluwak nuts, soaked in warm water then finely ground
2 lomboks (large red chillies), seeded and finely chopped
2 garlic cloves, finely chopped
1 teaspoon ground kencur (if not using fresh root above)

1. Pound all the bumbu ingredients to a paste using a pestle and mortar. If using fresh kencur root, do not add any ground kencur.
2. Heat the oil in a wok and gently fry the onion until softened. Add the bumbu paste and cook until fragrant.
3. Add the tomato, stock, salam leaf, fresh kencur (if using) and laos and stir well.
4. Once the tomato has softened, add the beef, season with salt (if desired) and simmer over a low heat for about 2 hours or until the meat is very tender.
5. Just before serving, add the creamed coconut and sugar. Stir to dissolve (add a little more water if it becomes too dry) then transfer to a serving dish and place the eggs alongside.

Babi Panggang Manado
roast pork, Manado style

In the city of Manado in northern Sulawesi there is a relatively large number of Christians. This explains the consumption of pork in mostly Muslim Indonesia. This roast pork belly dish is one of the local specialities and was originally cooked over a charcoal fire. To lower its calories use leaner pork; this works equally well.

500 g (1 lb 2 oz) loin or belly of pork (belly with rind)
1 teaspoon baking powder

For the bumbu:
3 lomboks (large red chillies), seeded and coarsely chopped (or 1 tablespoon Sambal Ulek, see page 238)
sea salt to taste
3 shallots, finely chopped
1 tablespoon tamarind water (dissolve a little tamarind puree in 1 tablespoon warm water)
2 garlic cloves, finely chopped
pinch of salt

1. Pound all the bumbu ingredients to a smooth paste using a pestle and mortar.
2. Rub the bumbu paste into the meat and leave to marinate for a minimum of 2 hours, preferably overnight.
3. Preheat the oven to 170°C (335°F / Gas 3).
4. Brush a roasting tin with oil. If using pork loin: place the meat in the roasting tin and brush lightly with baking powder. This will make it go crisp. Roast for approx. 45 minutes or until just done. If using pork belly: reduce the heat to 150°C (300°F / Gas 2) and roast the pork, skin side up, for approx. 1 hour or until crisp and cooked through.
5. Cut into thin slices just before serving.

Babi Chin
Chinese pork stew

The main condiment for 'Chinese pork' (the literal translation of 'babi chin') is tauco, a thick, salty puree made from fermented soy beans. Babi chin can also be made with spareribs or sliced pork belly.

4 shallots, finely chopped
1 garlic clove, crushed
2 tablespoons butter
1 lombok (large red chilli), seeded and finely chopped
1 tablespoon gula jawa (palm sugar), crushed
2 tablespoons kecap manis (sweet soy sauce)
1 tablespoon tauco (fermented soy bean paste)
500 g (1 lb 2 oz) boneless pork, cubed
200 ml (7 fl oz / 1 scant cup) tepid water
sea salt and pepper to taste

1. Gently fry the shallot and garlic in the butter until softened. Add the lombok and mix well.
2. Stir in the palm sugar, kecap manis and tauco, followed by the pork.
3. Pour in the water, bring to a simmer and reduce the heat to very low.
4. Simmer until most of the liquid has evaporated and the meat is tender and cooked through, for about 30 minutes. Stir regularly and add more water if it becomes too dry. Season with sea salt and pepper, then serve with rice or noodles.

Tip: Instead of using meat, this dish can also be prepared with tofu. Cut a block of tofu into cubes and fry these in hot oil until golden brown. Simmer the fried tofu in the sauce for 10 minutes.

Perkedel Pan
meat and potato pie

4 floury potatoes, cooked, peeled and mashed

250 g (9 oz) minced beef

250 g (9oz) minced pork

2 eggs

salt and pepper

dried breadcrumbs

25 g (1 oz) butter

For the bumbu:

4 shallots, finely chopped

2 garlic cloves, finely chopped

1 small stock cube, crumbled

1 heaped teaspoon (freshly grated) nutmeg

pinch of ground cloves

1. Preheat the oven to 180°C (355°F / Gas 4).
2. Put the mashed potato, minced meat, eggs and some salt and pepper in a bowl.
3. Pound all the bumbu ingredients to a paste and add to the potato mixture. Mix well with a fork or your hands.
4. Transfer the mixture to a greased ovenproof dish. Sprinkle with breadcrumbs and dot with butter before cooking in the oven for about 45 minutes or until golden, cooked through and crusty on top.

Tip: Spread a thin layer of kecap manis over the top of the dish after baking and return to the oven for 3–5 minutes.

Perkedel Tomat
tomatoes stuffed with minced meat

The word 'perkedel' derives from the Dutch word *'frikadel'*, which used to mean 'meatballs' (these days in The Netherlands it refers to a deep-fried sausage-like snack). In Indonesia the word 'perkedel' is used for a diversity of foods made with minced meat, fish or vegetables such as meatballs, corn or crab fritters, fishcakes, mince-stuffed vegetables and so on.

4 floury potatoes, cooked, peeled and mashed

250 g (9 oz) minced beef

250 g (9oz) minced pork

2 eggs

salt and pepper

8 beefsteak tomatoes

2 shallots, finely chopped

For the bumbu:

4 shallots, finely chopped

2 garlic cloves, finely chopped

1 small stock cube, crumbled

1 heaped teaspoon (freshly grated) nutmeg

1. Preheat the oven to 180°C (355°F / Gas 4).
2. Put the mashed potato, minced meat, eggs and some salt and pepper in a bowl.
3. Pound all the bumbu ingredients to a paste and add to the potato mixture. Mix well with a fork or your hands.
4. Cut the tops off the tomatoes, scoop out the core and seeds (preserving the juice) and place into a sieve over a bowl to catch every drop of juice. Put the tomato juice aside.
5. Stuff each tomato with an equal amount of the potato mixture and place into a greased baking dish. Drizzle with the tomato juice and sprinkle with shallot. Place the tops back on the tomatoes before baking in the oven for about 30 minutes or until the stuffing is cooked through.

Elephant intestines

The Bataks, the original inhabitants of Sumatra, are known for the rather strange things on their menus. On a small scale they still serve dogs and mice. 'Sop kaki kambing' is goat feet soup, in which, besides the legs, all the intestines and organs – including the genital organs – are prepared. 'Usus gajah' means 'Elephant intestines', but do not worry: it is simply a dish of fried beef with scrambled eggs.

Perkedel Goreng
fried potato and chilli meatballs

4 floury potatoes, cooked, peeled and mashed
250 g (9 oz) minced beef
250 g (9oz) minced pork
2 eggs
salt and pepper
dried breadcrumbs
vegetable oil for deep-frying

For the bumbu:
4 shallots, finely chopped
2 garlic cloves, finely chopped
1 lombok (large red chilli), seeded and finely chopped
1 small stock cube, crumbled
1 heaped teaspoon (freshly grated) nutmeg

1. Put the mashed potato, minced meat, eggs and some salt and pepper in a bowl.
2. Pound all the bumbu ingredients to a paste and add to the potato mixture. Mix well with a fork or your hands. Add some breadcrumbs if the mixture is too wet.
3. Shape the mixture into small rolls and coat with breadcrumbs.
4. Deep-fry the meatballs in hot oil in batches until golden and cooked through.

Daging Bumbu Bali
Balinese beef stew

Allow the beef to simmer very quietly for a few hours; it will be very tender and flavoursome. The tamarind's natural acidity actually helps to tenderise the beef by breaking down its fibres. Many people agree that this stew tastes even better the next day ...

2 tablespoons vegetable oil
500 g (1 lb 2 oz) stewing beef, cubed
2 kaffir lime leaves
2 salam leaves
1½ cm (½–1 in) piece fresh laos root (galangal)
2 cm (1 in) piece fresh ginger root
300 ml (10½ fl oz / 1¼ cup) water
2 tablespoons kecap manis (sweet soy sauce)
½ teaspoon tamarind puree

For the bumbu Bali:
3 garlic cloves, finely chopped
8 shallots, finely chopped
½ teaspoon trassi bakar (roasted dried shrimp paste)
2 kemiri (candlenuts), roasted (see tip on page 106)
2 lomboks (large red chillies), seeded and finely chopped
pinch of salt

1. Pound all the bumbu ingredients to a smooth paste using a pestle and mortar.
2. Gently fry the bumbu in the oil until fragrant, for about 1½ minutes. Add the meat and cook over a medium heat until lightly browned.
3. Add the kaffir lime and salam leaves, laos and ginger and cook for another minute or two.
4. Stir in the water, kecap manis and tamarind and simmer for about 2 hours or until the meat is tender but not quite falling apart. Stir regularly and add more water if it reduces too much. Serve with white rice.

Daging Bumbu Rujak
fragrant stewed beef with rujak spices

Rujak (sometimes spelled as 'roedjak') is a well-known Indonesian salad, usually made with green mangos and vegetables. The dressing is also popular as a base for other recipes, such as this beef stew. In restaurants the same dish is sometimes served with (fillet) steak and without coconut milk.

4 tablespoons vegetable oil
500 g (1 lb 2 oz) stewing beef
2 salam leaves
1½ piece fresh laos root (galangal)
1 lemongrass stalk, lightly bruised
300 ml (10½ fl oz / 1¼ cup) tepid water
1 teaspoon tamarind puree
1 teaspoon gula jawa (palm sugar)
50 g (1¾ oz) creamed coconut or 165 ml (5¾ fl oz / ⅔ cup) coconut milk
1 tablespoon tomato puree

For the bumbu rujak:
3 garlic cloves, finely chopped
8 shallots, finely chopped
½ teaspoon trassi bakar (roasted dried shrimp paste)
2 kemiri (candlenuts), roasted (see tip on page 106)
1 tablespoon Sambal Ulek (see page 238)
pinch of salt

1. Pound all the bumbu ingredients to a smooth paste using a pestle and mortar.
2. Heat 2 tablespoons of the oil in a wok, add the beef and fry in batches until lightly browned. Remove from the wok.
3. Heat the remaining oil in the wok and gently fry the bumbu paste until fragrant, for about 1½ minutes. Return the beef to the wok and mix well.
4. Add the salam leaves, laos and lemongrass and cook for another 1½ minutes.
5. Stir in the water, tamarind puree, palm sugar and half of the creamed coconut (or coconut milk) and bring to a simmer.
6. Lower the heat, add the remaining creamed coconut (or coconut milk) and the tomato puree and simmer for approx. 2 hours or until the meat is tender and the sauce has thickened. Check regularly and add more water if it reduces too much. Serve with white rice.

Dendeng Ragi
crispy pan-fried coconut beef

250 g (9 oz) freshly grated coconut or 100 g (3½ oz)
  desiccated coconut
4 tablespoons vegetable oil
salt and pepper to taste
500 g (1 lb 2 oz) (rump) steak, cut into strips
1 cm (½ in) piece fresh laos root (galangal)
2 salam leaves
2 kaffir lime leaves
100 ml (3 ½ fl oz / scant ½ cup) beef stock, warmed
sugar to taste

For the bumbu:
4 shallots, finely chopped
3 garlic cloves, finely chopped
2 teaspoons ground coriander
1 teaspoon ground cumin

1. If using desiccated coconut: sprinkle the coconut onto a platter and pour over just enough warm water to moisten. Allow to soak for 15 minutes or until most of the water has been absorbed.
2. Pound all bumbu ingredients to a smooth paste using a pestle and mortar.
3. Gently cook the bumbu paste in 2 tablespoons of oil in a wok until fragrant. Season with salt and pepper, then add the meat, laos, and salam and kaffir lime leaves. Cook briefly then stir in the stock. Simmer for about 2 minutes or until the meat is almost cooked through.
4. Once most of the liquid has evaporated add the coconut and cook over a low heat until the mixture has cooked dry. Stir regularly, taste and add sugar and more salt to taste.
5. Pour in the remaining oil, increase the heat to medium or high and toss until everything is very crisp without being burned.
6. Transfer to a sieve and drain. Serve with white rice.

Gulai Kambing
spicy goat or lamb curry

3 tablespoons vegetable oil
1 kg (2 lb 4 oz) goat meat or lamb, preferably on the bone
300 ml (10½ fl oz / 1¼ cup) water
1½ tablespoons tomato puree
1 salam leaf
1½ cm (1 in) piece fresh laos root (galangal)
1 lemongrass stalk, lightly bruised
½ teaspoon tamarind puree
1 kaffir lime leaf
50 g (1¾ oz) creamed coconut, crumbled

For the bumbu:
3 garlic cloves, finely chopped
3 shallots, finely chopped
2 lomboks (large red chillies), seeded and finely chopped
2 rawits (bird's eye chillies), finely chopped
1 tablespoon ground coriander
1 teaspoon ground turmeric
1 teaspoon ground cumin
3 cm (1½ in) piece fresh ginger root (or ½ teaspoon ground ginger)
2 cloves
½ teaspoon (freshly grated) nutmeg
1 teaspoon ground cinnamon
½ teaspoon trassi (dried shrimp paste)

1. Pound all the bumbu ingredients to a smooth paste using a pestle and mortar.
2. Gently fry the bumbu in the oil until fragrant, for about 2–3 minutes.
3. Add the meat, increase the heat and fry until browned.
4. Pour in the water, add the tomato puree, salam leaf, laos, lemongrass, tamarind puree and kaffir lime leaf and simmer for 1–1½ hours.
5. Stir in the creamed coconut and dissolve. Allow to simmer for another 30 minutes or until the meat is very tender.

Dendeng Ragi

'In Java the beef for dendeng ragi was beaten flat, spiced, then allowed to dry in the sun. Afterwards we fried it in a little butter or oil together with the grated coconut,' says one Indonesian cook. Dendeng ragi makes a great side dish for any 'wet dish', such as a sayur (soupy stew).

Gulai Kambing

'Kambing' means goat meat. Because of its limited availability it's often replaced with lamb. It's worth trying to find goat meat though, as it's surprisingly mild in flavour (milder than lamb for instance) but very tasty. Gulai is directly inspired by Indian curries, hence its fiery hot nature. True gulai aficionados claim that this curry can never be hot enough, so don't hold back on the chillies.

Rendang
authentic Sumatran stewed beef

While the meat is simmering away, the water in the coconut milk evaporates, bringing the coconut oil slowly to the surface, and the stewing gradually becomes frying. Classic Sumatran rendang will stay on the stove until it's cooked totally dry and the solids in the coconut milk have formed a kind of paste, which sticks to the meat. If you prefer your rendang with sauce, simply take the pan off the stove as soon as the meat is tender. At this stage your stew is called rendang basah (wet rendang).

750 g (1 lb 10 oz) stewing beef, cut into 2 cm (1 in) cubes
300 ml (10½ oz / 1¼ cup) beef stock
125 g (4½ oz / ⅔ block) creamed coconut, crumbled
2 salam leaves
2 kaffir lime leaves
2½ cm (1½ in) piece fresh laos root (galangal)
1 lemongrass stalk, lightly bruised

For the bumbu:
3 garlic cloves, finely chopped
1 teaspoon trassi (dried shrimp paste)
5 rawits (bird's eye chillies), finely chopped
½ teaspoon ground turmeric
1 tablespoon vegetable oil

1. Pound all the bumbu ingredients to a smooth paste using a pestle and mortar.
2. Marinate the meat for a minimum of 2 hours in the bumbu.
3. Bring the stock to a simmer, add the creamed coconut and dissolve.
4. Add the meat and marinade, along with all remaining ingredients and simmer uncovered for 1½–2 hours over a very low heat. Stir regularly and add more water if necessary. The rendang is ready when the beef is very tender and the sauce has reduced completely.

Daging Semur
beef simmered in kecap sauce

Stewing is the most popular method of preparing beef in Indonesia. Rare or medium-rare meat is hardly ever eaten. Serve this stew with a generous spoonful of sambal to obtain the right balance between spicy and sweet.

50 g (1¾ oz) butter

500 g (2 lb 2 oz) stewing beef, cut into 2 cm (1 in) cubes

500 ml (17 fl oz / 2 cups) beef stock, warmed (not hot)

3 tablespoons kecap manis (sweet soy sauce)

2 cloves

salt, pepper and sugar to taste

For the bumbu:

8 shallots, finely chopped

3 garlic cloves, finely chopped

½ teaspoon (freshly grated) nutmeg

1. Melt half the butter in a wok, add the beef and fry until browned. Remove from the wok and set aside.
2. Pound all the bumbu ingredients to a smooth paste using a pestle and mortar.
3. Gently fry the bumbu in the remaining butter in the wok until fragrant.
4. Return the beef to the wok and add enough stock to just cover.
5. Stir in the kecap manis and cloves and simmer for about 2 hours or until the meat is tender.
6. Remove the cloves from the wok and add salt, pepper and sugar to taste.

Serundeng Daging
dry-fried sweet and spicy coconut beef

Serundeng daging is a type of side dish with the specific purpose of bringing balance to a meal or rice table by adding crunch. Other side dishes serving the same purpose are Sambal Goreng Kering Kentang (see page 96) and tahu goreng (fried tofu).

1 kg (2 lb 4 oz) stewing beef, cut into 2 cm (1 in) cubes

2 salam leaves

150 g (5 oz) desiccated coconut

salt to taste

For the bumbu:

8 shallots, finely chopped

3 garlic cloves, finely chopped

2 teaspoons ground coriander

1 teaspoon ground cumin

1 tablespoon gula jawa (palm sugar)

1. Pound all the bumbu ingredients to a smooth paste using a pestle and mortar.
2. Add the meat and salam leaves to the bumbu paste and mix well. Transfer to a large saucepan with a thin layer of water poured into it and simmer for approx. 2 hours or until the meat is very tender. Stir regularly and add more water if it becomes too dry.
3. Stir in the coconut, increase the heat slightly and continue to stir-fry until everything is browned, dry and aromatic without being burned.

Tip: Perk up this dish by adding a handful of peeled and cubed waxy potatoes and some su-un noodles about 10 minutes towards the end of the cooking time.

Soy sauce: the world's most popular sauce

Indonesian cuisine would never be the same without soy sauce ('kecap' in modern Indonesian) with its unique, complex smell and taste. At the basis of this versatile sauce is an ancient creation.

Soy sauce was invented in China about three thousand years ago. The Chinese left soybeans with salt and water in earthenware jars in the warm sun. Inside the jars a wondrous thing happened: there was a dark brown, delicious smelling paste. The best soy sauce today is still made in a similar way. Steamed soybeans are mixed with water, salt and special fungi, and then left for a few months. In a process as enigmatic as making wine, protein is converted into amino acid and starch into sugar. After pressing and filtering, a clear, deep, amber-coloured sauce appears. There are major differences between soy sauces from different Asian food cultures. This is partly due to the addition of certain grains, more or less salt, or a longer or shorter time of maturing. The main Indonesian soy sauce types are kecap manis (sweet), kecap asin (salty) and kecap sedang (sweet–salty). Kecap manis, the type that is frequently on the table, generally has additional seasonings added to it – thus for the Indonesians, it is the best soy sauce in the world.

Soy sauce and ketchup

Around the beginning of the eighteenth century Europeans brought home kecap from Asia and tried to recreate it – for instance with walnuts, beans and mushrooms. Their greatest success was a version made from tomatoes, which we now know as … ketchup!

Satay

These delicious marinated and roasted pieces of meat threaded onto bamboo skewers are probably the most well-known and loved Indonesian dish in the world. Instead of bamboo, satay skewers are sometimes made of the hard inner grain of palm leaves, which give a special flavour. Indonesians use all sorts of meat for satay: chicken, beef and pork, lamb or goat, and also fish, prawns or squid, or even tripe and liver ... The marinade almost always contains kunyit (kunir, or turmeric) and there is usually a spicy sauce to accompany the meat, usually made from freshly ground peanuts. But the most important ingredient is probably the charcoal fire on which the satay is grilled. Whether you buy satay skewers on the street or eat them in an expensive restaurant, the smoked aroma gives them that authentic taste.

Sate Daging
skewered spicy beef

Choose tender beef cuts for this type of satay such as sirloin, rib eye, top loin or tenderloin.

500 g (1 lb 2 oz) tender boneless beef, cubed
wooden skewers, soaked in cold water for 30 minutes

For the marinade:
1 onion, finely chopped
2 garlic cloves, finely chopped
2 lomboks (large red chillies), seeded and finely chopped
   (or 1 tablespoon Sambal Ulek, see page 238)
2 kemiri (candlenuts), roasted (see tip on page 106),
   then finely pounded
small piece of fresh ginger root, finely chopped
1 heaped teaspoon ground coriander
½ teaspoon ground turmeric
1 teaspoon gula jawa (palm sugar), crushed
1 salam leaf
1 kaffir lime leaf
sea salt to taste
2 tablespoons vegetable oil

1. For the marinade, pound together the onion, garlic, lombok (or sambal), kemiri and ginger using a pestle and mortar. Transfer to a bowl and add the remaining marinade ingredients and mix well.
2. Add the beef, mix to ensure all the cubes are well coated, cover and leave to marinade for a minimum of 2 hours.
3. Thread the meat onto the skewers.
4. Cook the skewers on a hot charcoal barbecue (or grill them in the oven) for approx. 4 minutes or until cooked to your liking. Turn them often and baste regularly with leftover marinade. Serve with Simple Kecap Sauce (see page 199).

Sate Ayam
best-ever chicken satay

The tamarind and lemon in this marinade make the chicken wonderfully juicy and tender, while the kecap manis gives a delicious sweet and savoury flavour.

400 g (14 oz) chicken breast, cut into 2 cm (1 in) cubes
wooden skewers, soaked in cold water for 30 minutes

For the marinade:
3 garlic cloves, finely chopped
5 tablespoons kecap manis (sweet soy sauce)
1 tablespoon lemon juice
1 teaspoon tamarind puree
1 teaspoon gula jawa (palm sugar)
salt to taste
1 tablespoon vegetable oil

1. Place all the marinade ingredients in a bowl. Stir to combine, then add the chicken, mixing well to ensure all the cubes are well coated. Cover and marinate for a minimum of 2 hours.
2. Thread 4–6 pieces of chicken onto each skewer.
3. Cook the skewers on a hot charcoal barbecue (or grill them in the oven) until golden and cooked through. Turn them often and baste regularly with leftover marinade. The skewers should be taken off the grill immediately when cooked through to prevent them from drying out. Serve with Peanut Sauce (see opposite).

Peanut Sauce

a dash of milk • ½ jar (175 g / 6 oz) peanut butter •
2 teaspoons Sambal Ulek (see page 238) • 1 tablespoon
gula jawa (palm sugar) • 1 onion, halved • 1 garlic clove,
crushed • ¼ lemon, quartered • pinch of salt •
1 teaspoon tamarind puree • 3 generous tablespoons
kecap manis (sweet soy sauce) • water

1. Pour a thin layer of milk (approx. 1 cm / ½ in) into a
   saucepan, place over a low heat and stir in the peanut
   butter.
2. Add the remaining ingredients, apart from the water.
   Heat through, stirring all the time while adding enough
   water (a splash at a time) to give a nice smooth sauce.
3. Remove the pieces of lemon and onion just before
   serving.

Sate Kambing
skewered goat meat or lamb
with kecap sauce

Specialist halal butchers sometimes sell goat meat. Surprisingly, it tastes milder than lamb, which is a good replacement. Both goat and lamb are well-flavoured meats and marinating is therefore not necessary. A little basting with kecap manis during the cooking process is all they need. This satay is traditionally served with a simple kecap sauce. Alternatively after cooking you can dip the skewers into the sauce and return them to the grill for 30 seconds.

500 g (1 lb 2 oz) lean goat meat or lamb, cut into 2 cm (1 in) cubes
wooden skewers, soaked in cold water for 30 minutes
salt

For the kecap sauce:
2 shallots, finely chopped
4 garlic cloves, finely chopped
2 tablespoons kecap asin or Chinese soy sauce
2 tablespoons kecap manis (sweet soy sauce)
1 lombok (large red chilli), seeded and finely chopped
1 tablespoon lemon juice to taste (optional)

1. Thread the meat onto the skewers and sprinkle with salt.
2. For the sauce, combine all the ingredients in a bowl. Set aside.
3. Cook the skewers on a hot charcoal barbecue (or grill them in the oven) until browned and cooked through. Turn them often and, if using lamb, be careful not to overcook as it dries out easily.
4. Serve with the kecap sauce.

Sate Manis
sweet beef satay

This sweet and spicy satay is usually eaten without any sauce. If sauce is a must, serve it with Simple Kecap Sauce (see opposite).

500 g (1 lb 2 oz) tender boneless beef, cut into 2 cm
  (1 in) cubes
wooden skewers, soaked in cold water for 30 minutes

For the marinade:

3 shallots, finely chopped
3 garlic cloves, finely chopped
1 teaspoon ground coriander
1 teaspoon ground laos (galangal)
1 teaspoon ground cumin
1 teaspoon ground ginger
1 teaspoon gula jawa (palm sugar), crushed
1 tablespoon tamarind water
1 generous teaspoon lemon juice
2 tablespoons kecap manis (sweet soy sauce)
salt to taste (optional)

1. For the marinade, pound the shallots and garlic to a paste using a pestle and mortar. Add the remaining marinade ingredients and stir well.
2. Spoon the marinade over the beef, turning to coat well. Cover and chill for a minimum of 2 hours.
3. Thread the beef onto the skewers.
4. Cook the skewers on a hot charcoal barbecue (or grill them in the oven) until cooked through or to your liking. Turn them often and baste regularly with leftover marinade.

Sate Pentul Ayam
minced chicken satay

You can replace the chicken with minced beef or even minced pork, the latter being a Bali favourite. The spice paste (bumbu) remains the same regardless of the type of meat.

500 g (1 lb 2 oz) minced chicken breast (you can do this
  in the food processor)
1 egg
½ teaspoon tamarind puree
salt to taste
flour or fine dried breadcrumbs
8–10 thick bamboo skewers or lemongrass stalks

For the bumbu:

2 kemiri (candlenuts), roasted (see tip on page 106), then
  finely pounded
½ teaspoon trassi bakar (roasted dried shrimp paste)
5 shallots, finely chopped
½ teaspoon ground cumin
½ teaspoon ground coriander
50 g (1¾ oz) desiccated coconut or 1 tablespoon
  creamed coconut
2 garlic cloves, finely chopped
1 lombok (large red chilli), seeded and finely chopped
  (or 1 teaspoon Sambal Ulek, see page 238)

1. Pound all the bumbu ingredients to a smooth paste using a pestle and mortar.
2. Combine the bumbu paste, minced chicken, egg, tamarind puree and salt and mix well. Add some breadcrumbs or a little flour if the mixture is too wet.
3. Shape the meat mixture into small sausage-like shapes and mould around the skewers. If using lemongrass: remove the outer leaves of each stalk and cut the thinner end at an angle to make skewers. Mould the meat around the stalks.
4. Cook the skewers on a hot charcoal barbecue (or grill them in the oven) for approx. 8 minutes or until golden and cooked through, turning them carefully from time to time.

Simple Kecap Sauce

3 shallots, finely chopped • 1 garlic clove, finely chopped •
1–2 tablespoons lemon juice • 150 ml (5 fl oz / ⅔ cup)
kecap manis (sweet soy sauce) • pinch of salt • 3 rawits
(bird's eye chillies), finely chopped (optional)

1. Mix all the ingredients in a bowl and add salt to
   taste. Add the rawits if you like it hot.

Sate Padang
meat in spicy sauce, Padang style

Originally, Padang-style satay is made with beef offal such as tongue, heart, liver, tripe and brains. However, non-Muslim Indonesians prepare this type of satay preferably with pork, as described in the recipe below. Of course, there is nothing preventing you from preparing this satay in the original way of the Minangkabau (the first inhabitants of Padang in Sumatra) with offal or a mixture of meat and offal. Allow the sauce to reduce until very thick or use a little of the cooking water of the rice to thicken it.

3 tablespoons vegetable oil
5 shallots, finely chopped
3 garlic cloves, finely chopped
500 g (1 lb 2 oz) lean pork or beef/veal offal (e.g. heart, tripe, tongue etc.), cubed
2 teaspoons ground coriander
2 teaspoons ground turmeric
1 teaspoon ground cumin
1 small piece of fresh ginger root
1 small piece of fresh laos root (galangal)
1 lombok (large red chilli), seeded and finely chopped (or 1 tablespoon Sambal Ulek, see page 238)
pinch of salt
2 tablespoons (rice) vinegar
150 ml (5 fl oz / ⅔ cup) tepid water
1 tablespoon creamed coconut, crumbled

1. Heat the oil, add the shallot and garlic and gently fry until translucent.
2. Add the meat and brown on all sides.
3. Add the ground spices, ginger, laos, lombok and salt, then cook for about 1½ minutes, stirring all the time. Pour in the vinegar and tepid water.
4. Add the creamed coconut and stir until dissolved. Lower the heat and leave to simmer for approx. 1 hour or until the meat is tender and most of the fluid has evaporated. Serve with plain rice or lontong (see page 74).

Tip: Sate padang is usually served unskewered and prepared in a wok or frying pan. For barbecued sate padang, just follow the recipe but skip step 2. Simmer the sauce until reduced down completely. Allow to cool, then marinate the meat in this mixture for 1 hour. Thread the meat onto skewers and cook on a hot (charcoal) barbecue.

Sate Lilit Ikan
skewered Balinese fish cakes

This delicious Balinese satay is made of pureed fish (sometimes in combination with seafood such as crab meat and prawns) and spices, moulded onto fresh lemongrass stalks. 'Lilit' means 'turning' in Balinese, and this turning of the skewers needs to be done with care ensuring the fragile satay doesn't break. To baste the satay with coconut milk as it grills, use the thick end of a smashed lemongrass stalk as a brush. This adds the taste of fresh lemongrass to the satay.

300 g (10½ oz) firm fish fillets (e.g. tuna, mackerel or sword fish), coarsely chopped
8 lemongrass stalks, trimmed and thinner ends cut at an angle to make skewers (+ 1 extra stalk for basting, optional)
dried breadcrumbs or flour (optional)
coconut milk for basting
crispy fried onions, to garnish

For the bumbu:
3 garlic cloves, finely chopped
3 shallots, finely chopped
2 kemiri (candlenuts), roasted (see tip on page 106), then finely pounded
¼ teaspoon trassi (dried shrimp paste)
4 kaffir lime leaves
2 tablespoons coconut milk
3 teaspoons gula jawa (palm sugar)
2 teaspoons tamarind water
1 lemongrass stalk
1 lombok (large red chilli), seeded and finely chopped
1 teaspoon ground turmeric
1 teaspoon ground ginger
1 teaspoon ground laos (galangal)

1. For the bumbu, pound the garlic, shallot, kemiri and trassi to a paste using a pestle and mortar. Transfer to a food processor, add the remaining bumbu ingredients and pulse briefly.
2. Add the fish and blend to a smooth, dough-like mixture. Cover and refrigerate for 2 hours until firm.
3. Mould approx. 1 tablespoon of fish mixture around each lemongrass stalk (add some breadcrumbs or a little flour if the mixture is too wet).
4. Cook the skewers on a hot charcoal barbecue (or grill them in the oven) until golden and cooked through, turning them carefully from time to time. Baste with coconut milk regularly during grilling to prevent burning.
5. Garnish with fried onions and serve with plain rice and a vegetable dish such as Tumis Kangkung (see page 122).

Sate Tahu
fried tofu skewers

This vegetarian satay has become very popular all over Southeast Asia. Serve with either Simple Kecap Sauce or Peanut Sauce (pages 199 and 195).

375 g (13 oz) tofu
vegetable oil for frying
wooden skewers, soaked in cold water for 30 minutes

For the marinade:
2 tablespoons lemon juice
2 tablespoons kecap manis (sweet soy sauce)
1 tablespoon gula jawa (palm sugar)
1½ teaspoons ground coriander
1 garlic clove, finely chopped
salt and pepper

1. Cut the tofu into 1½ cm (½ in) thick slices and place into a saucepan. Cook in plenty boiling water for 10 minutes. Drain and cool.
2. Mix all the ingredients for the marinade and season with salt and pepper.
3. Cut the tofu into 2 cm (1 in) cubes. Pour the marinade over the tofu, cover and chill for about 1 hour.
4. Thread the tofu cubes onto the skewers.
5. Heat a generous amount of oil in a frying pan and brown the tofu on all sides. Alternatively, cook the oil-brushed tofu skewers on a hot (charcoal) barbecue.

Sate Udang Pedas
spicy prawn satay

In spite of the chillies, the flavour of this prawn satay is too delicate to eat with peanut sauce. Serve these skewers with a (spicy) tomato sauce instead.

300 g (10½ oz) peeled and de-veined raw prawns
wood skewers, soaked in cold water for 30 minutes

For the marinade:
2 tablespoons vegetable oil
2 garlic cloves, finely chopped
3 lomboks (large red chillies), seeded and finely chopped
½ teaspoon trassi (dried shrimp paste)
1 tablespoon lemon juice
2 kemiri (candlenuts), roasted (see tip on page 106), then finely pounded
1 teaspoon hot paprika
pinch of salt

1. First make the marinade. Heat the oil, add the garlic, lombok and trassi and gently fry for about 3 minutes.
2. Place the remaining marinade ingredients into a bowl, add the fried lombok mixture and stir well.
3. Add the prawns, give it a good stir, cover and refrigerate for 1 hour to let the flavours develop.
4. Thread the prawns onto the skewers and cook on a hot charcoal barbecue (or grill them in the oven) for about 1–2 minutes on either side or until just cooked through.

Sate Babi
world-famous pork satay with peanut sauce

The classical Balinese pork satay tastes best when served with freshly made peanut sauce, cakes of cold lontong sticky rice for mopping up the sauce (see page 74), crispy fried onions and sweet and sour pickles (acar). For the ultimate smoky flavour and lightly charred edges, cook the skewers on a charcoal barbecue. They should cook quite fast so watch closely, turn often and do not burn.

2 garlic cloves, finely chopped
4 cm (2 in) piece of fresh ginger root, grated
(or 1 teaspoon ground ginger)
1 small stock cube (for 200 ml / 7 fl oz / 1 scant cup), crumbled
3 tablespoons kecap manis (sweet soy sauce)
1 teaspoon ground coriander
juice ½ lemon
750 g lean boneless pork, cut into 2 cm (1 in) cubes
wooden skewers, soaked in cold water for 30 minutes
handful of crispy fried onions, to garnish

For the peanut sauce:
500 ml (17 fl oz / 2 cups) stock or water
1 lombok (large red chilli), seeded and very finely chopped
½ jar (175 g / 6 oz) peanut butter
1 tablespoon rice vinegar
1 heaped tablespoon gula jawa (palm sugar), crushed
dash of kecap manis (sweet soy sauce)

1. Pound the garlic, ginger and crumbled stock cube to a paste using a pestle and mortar. Add the kecap manis, coriander and lemon juice and mix well. Rub the paste all over the pork and marinate for about 30 minutes.
2. For the sauce, bring the stock or water with the lombok to the boil. Take off the heat, add the peanut butter and stir until it has completely dissolved.
3. Season the sauce with the remaining ingredients.
4. Thread the pork onto the skewers (about 4 cubes on each skewer).
5. Cook the skewers on a hot charcoal barbecue (or use a griddle pan or oven grill) until nicely browned and cooked through.
6. Place 2–3 skewers on each plate, spoon over some peanut sauce and top with crispy fried onions.

Street food: freshly prepared day and night

Some Indonesians 'do not eat to live, but live to eat'. In the cities you can buy food from little food stalls day and night and you find them literally on every street corner. Office staff, families and businessmen will get a quick lunch of soto (soup), an evening dinner with nasi or tasty snacks such as satay or banana fritter.

Along the main roads and in the cities you will find small stalls with jajanan (small savoury or sweet snacks) and drinks of sugar cane, fruit or fresh young coconut, which you drink with a straw. They call these food stalls *kaki lima* or 'five feet', meaning three 'feet' of the cart from which they sell the snacks plus two feet for the vendor. Street vendors usually specialise in one or two dishes they have prepared in advance or purchased from someone who prepared them at home. They often sing or call out while wheeling their cart through the streets to market their wares. Overall they are very inexpensive. *Warungs* are small eateries on the street where the seller usually prepares the food in front of you. These dining places are more popular among the local population than *rumah makans* (cafes) and restaurants. Indonesians mainly eat outdoors for convenience; for special or festive occasions they cook a large dinner at home. For example, you can eat a fresh spring roll, noodle soup with fresh vegetables, or rujak made from fresh fruit and vegetables in a spicy sauce. However, you will have to find a seat on one of the wooden benches or at a plastic table, because only horses eat standing up. As the proverb says: *'Makannya seperti kuda'* or 'Eat like a horse.'

Fish and seafood

Not all Indonesians eat rice, but they all eat fish. It could not really be otherwise in a country that is made up of islands and islets, surrounded by seas and oceans. Many ingredients that give Indonesian dishes their flavour are based on fish or crustaceans – trassi and petis udang, for example, are both pastes of (fermented) shrimps, which give dishes with fish, vegetables and also meat a

spicy aroma. There is also the complex-tasting kecap ikan, a sort of fermented fish sauce. Also dried fish and small fish are eaten often; with rice and sambal these make a simple meal. For festive occasions, there are dishes with expensive ingredients such as crab, large prawns or crayfish. And of course there is a wealth of fresh fish dishes, fried, steamed, deep fried or in a delicious sambal or sauce.

Ikan Putih Goreng
crispy fried white fish

This crispy fried fish is fabulous when served with a freshly made sweet and spicy sambal such as Sambal Gandaria (see page 244). You can use any white fish fillet for ikan putih goreng, but haddock, tilapia or grey mullet work particularly well.

110 g (4 oz / 1 cup) flour, sieved

120 ml (4 fl oz / ½ cup) water

1 teaspoon salt

1 teaspoon garlic powder (optional)

vegetable oil for deep-frying

1 fresh haddock fillet or other firm white fish, cleaned and cut into 5 cm (2 in) pieces (bones removed as much as possible)

1. Combine flour, water, salt and garlic powder, if using, into a smooth batter.
2. Heat a generous layer of oil in a wok (or deep fat fryer).
3. Dip the fish into the batter and lower into the hot oil using a spoon. Deep-fry for a couple of minutes or until golden and crisp. Drain on paper towel.

Ikan Goreng
fried tamarind fish

The sour, fresh taste of tamarind complements fish perfectly. Not surprisingly, you'll often find the two together in Indonesian cuisine, a bit like lemon and fish in Western cuisines. In the recipe below, the tamarind also gives the fish a nice crunchy layer. If you want, you can add extra condiments to the marinade such as lemongrass, garlic or chillies. Choose any fish you like, but make sure it's firm.

1 tablespoon tamarind puree, dissolved in 250 ml (9 fl oz / 1 cup) water with 1 teaspoon salt

1 large mackerel or snapper (or use 500 g / 1 lb 2 oz tuna fillet instead)

vegetable oil for deep-frying

1. Pour the tamarind water over the fish and leave to stand for 30 minutes.
2. Heat a generous layer of oil in a wok.
3. Pat the fish dry with paper towel and lower carefully into the hot oil. Fry until browned and crisp on all sides. Remove from the wok using a slotted spoon and drain on paper towel. Serve straight away.

Ikan Pindang Kuning
Maluku-style fish with chillies and tomatoes

This fish dish originates in the Moluccas (Maluku) and Irian Jaya, where it is traditionally made with tuna and eaten with papeda, a jelly-like sago porridge. Sago is a starchy product extracted from the pith of the sago palm. In many parts of Maluku, sago is actually more common than rice. Although tuna is the traditional choice, you can use any other firm fish.

small piece of fresh ginger root

1 garlic clove, finely chopped

½ teaspoon ground turmeric

3 tablespoons vegetable oil

1 onion, thinly sliced

2 lomboks (large red chillies), halved lengthwise, seeded and cut in two

5 tomatoes, coarsely chopped

500 ml (17 fl oz / 2 cups) vegetable or chicken stock

2 teaspoons salt

1 tablespoon (rice) vinegar

small handful of celery leaves, coarsely chopped

8 pieces (approx. 500 g / 2 lb 2 oz) of firm fish fillet (e.g. red snapper or tuna)

crispy fried onions, to garnish

1. In a pestle and mortar, pound the ginger and garlic with the turmeric to a paste.
2. Heat the oil in a wok and fry the onion until golden. Add the ginger paste, the lombok and tomato and cook, stirring all the time, until the tomato has softened.
3. Pour in the stock, bring to the boil and add the salt, vinegar and celery leaves. Slide the fish fillets into the wok and simmer for about 15 minutes or until the fish is cooked through. Serve with rice and top with crispy fried onions.

Tip: Ginger skin can be easily removed after rinsing the root for 30 seconds under a running hot tap.

Sambal Goreng Udang
hot and spicy prawns

There are various recipes for this spicy prawn dish, most of which contain petai beans. Fresh petai beans look similar to broad beans and have a powerful odour, which has gained them the nickname 'smelly beans'. Don't let this scare you off though, because it's the petai beans that give this dish its delicious, unique taste.

3 tablespoons vegetable oil

300 g (10½ oz) raw, peeled and de-veined (medium or large size) prawns

4 petai beans, halved lengthwise

1 salam leaf

2–3 cm (1 in) piece fresh laos root (galangal)

1 tablespoon tamarind puree

1 tablespoon gula jawa (palm sugar)

25 g (1 oz) creamed coconut

2 kaffir lime leaves

1 lemongrass stalk, lightly bruised

100 ml (3 ½ fl oz / scant ½ cup) chicken stock

For the bumbu:

4 shallots, finely chopped

3 lomboks (large red chillies), seeded and finely chopped

2 garlic cloves, finely chopped

1 teaspoon trassi (dried shrimp paste)

½ teaspoon salt

1. Pound all the bumbu ingredients to a paste using a pestle and mortar.

2. Heat the oil in a wok, add the bumbu paste and fry gently until fragrant, for about 1–2 minutes.

3. Add the prawns and petai beans, stir well and fry for 1 minute over a medium heat.

4. Add the salam leaf, laos, tamarind puree, palm sugar, creamed coconut, kaffir lime leaves and lemongrass and stir well.

5. Pour in the stock, bring to a simmer and reduce the heat. Cook for about 3 minutes. Add a little tepid water if the sauce reduces more than desired.

Acar Ikan
fried fish in sweet and sour sauce

1 portion Ikan Putih Goreng (see page 214) or 2 battered
    fish fillets from the fishmonger
3 kemiri (candlenuts), roasted (see tip on page 106),
    then finely pounded
3 garlic cloves, finely chopped
2 teaspoons ground turmeric
vegetable oil for frying
4 tablespoons (rice) vinegar
1 tablespoon sugar + extra to taste
125 ml (4 fl oz / ½ cup) tepid (chicken) stock
2 small onions, coarsely chopped
½ red capsicum, coarsely chopped
salt and pepper

1. Place the fish in a preheated oven at 150°C (300°F / Gas 2) for 10 minutes or until heated through.
2. Meanwhile, using a pestle and mortar, finely pound the kemiri, garlic and turmeric to a paste.
3. Heat a little oil in a wok, add the paste and fry until fragrant.
4. Stir in the vinegar, then add the sugar and stock. Bring to the boil, add the onion and capsicum and reduce to a simmer.
5. Season the sauce with salt, pepper and extra sugar. It should have a nicely balanced sweet and sour taste.
6. Remove the fish from the oven and place on a heated serving platter. Spoon over the sauce and serve immediately.

Pepesan
steamed mackerel wrapped in banana leaf

2 mackerels, cleaned
3 tablespoons vegetable oil
1 onion, finely chopped
3 garlic cloves, finely chopped
4 lomboks (large red chillies), seeded and finely chopped
    (or 1 tablespoon Sambal Ulek, see page 238)
5 kemiri (candlenuts), roasted (see tip on page 106),
    then finely pounded
3 kaffir lime leaves
½ lemon, coarsely chopped
250 g (9 oz) tomatoes, pounded to a paste using a pestle
    and mortar
1 salam leaf
1 teaspoon ground laos (galangal)
1 teaspoon ground turmeric
1 cm (½ in) cube trassi (dried shrimp paste), crumbled
1 tablespoon salt
1 small stock cube (for 200 ml / 7 fl oz / 1 scant cup)
banana leaves (or aluminium foil)
2 lemongrass stalks, lightly bruised

1. Mix all the ingredients, except the mackerel, the oil, the banana leaves and the lemongrass, in a large bowl.
2. Heat 3 tablespoons of oil in a wok, add the mixture and fry gently until fragrant, for about 3 minutes.
3. Fill the cavities of the mackerel with some of the mixture and place each fish on top of a banana leaf (or a large sheet of aluminium foil). Spread the remaining mixture over the top of the fish.
4. Fold each stalk of lemongrass in half and place on top of the fish. Wrap neatly into parcels, bringing the sides of the banana leaves (or foil) together and turning in the ends. Cover and chill for 2 hours.
5. Preheat the oven to 180°C (350°F / Gas 4).
6. Cook the fish parcels for approx. 30 minutes in the oven.

Pepesan

In the original recipe, the banana leaf packages are first steamed and then roasted. Preparing them in the oven however, is much more convenient and gives an equally good result. Choose a fatty, firm type of fish such as mackerel. Smoked mackerel also works well but make sure to reduce the cooking time in the oven to 15-20 minutes.

Rica-rica Udang
stir-fried prawns in chilli and tomato sauce

Rica-rica spice paste with chillies, ginger and tomato is a speciality of the Minahasa tribe from Sulawesi. It forms the base of dishes with fish, chicken, beef and pork, or, like the recipe below, with juicy prawns. To prevent the prawns from becoming tough, make sure to not overcook them.

1 onion, finely chopped
2 garlic cloves, finely chopped
4 tablespoons vegetable oil
2 tomatoes, diced
2 lomboks (large red chillies), seeded and thinly sliced
3 cm (1¼ in) piece fresh ginger root, grated
pinch of salt
1 tablespoon sugar
100 ml (3½ fl oz / scant ½ cup) water
1 tablespoon tomato puree
250 g (9 oz) peeled large raw (Chinese) prawns

1. Using a pestle and mortar, pound the onion and garlic to a paste. Heat two tablespoons of oil in a wok or large frying pan, add the paste and gently cook for a minute or two.

2. Add the tomatoes, stir well then add the lombok, ginger, salt and sugar.

3. Pour in the water, bring to a simmer and cook for 5 minutes.

4. Add the tomato puree and continue to simmer for a few more minutes.

5. Meanwhile, heat the remaining oil in another wok, add the prawns and stir-fry until pink and just cooked, for about 1–2 minutes. Transfer to a serving dish and pour over the sauce.

Cumi-cumi
stewed squid in spicy sauce

Octopus crops up regularly on the Indonesian menu, whether baked, grilled, fried or steamed. There is even a speciality of octopus cooked in its own ink. 'Cumi-cumi' means 'squid'. For the recipe below you can also use baby squid. The squid is first boiled in water until tender, then cooked briefly with the herbs and spices. Alternatively, you can pre-cook the squid for a shorter period of time (until just about half-done) and allow for a longer stewing time in the sauce.

1 squid (or 6 baby squid), thawed if frozen
2 tablespoons vegetable oil
2 garlic cloves, finely chopped
2 onions, finely chopped
1 lombok (large red chilli), seeded and finely chopped
1 teaspoon trassi (dried shrimp paste), crumbled
1 teaspoon ground coriander
1 salam leaf
½ teaspoon ground laos (galangal)

1. Pull the tentacles away from the body of the squid, removing the ink sac and entrails. Carefully remove and discard the plastic-looking backbone by pulling it out of the body, then rinse the body.

2. Place the squid in a large pan of salted boiling water and cook until tender, for about 50 minutes. (Check if it's done by inserting a knife gently into the thickest part of the squid. You should be able to do this easily.) Drain, reserving the cooking liquid, and cut into pieces.

3. Heat the oil in a wok, add the garlic, onion, lombok and trassi and fry gently until softened.

4. Add the remaining ingredients and stir well.

5. Lower the heat and add the pieces of squid. Pour in enough of the reserved cooking liquid to cover and simmer for 5 minutes. Stir once then serve with rice.

Ikan Mangut
coconut-simmered fish

Mangut is a Javanese dish of coconut-simmered (smoked) fish, usually smoked sting-ray (ikan pari). In other parts of the world, Indonesians often use smoked mackerel or even ordinary battered white fish.

2 tablespoons vegetable oil

2 salam leaves

1 x 165 ml (5½ fl oz) small can coconut milk

1 teaspoon tamarind puree

2 smoked mackerels, skin removed

(or 1 portion Ikan Putih Goreng, see page 214)

For the bumbu:

6 lomboks (large red chillies), seeded and soaked for 10 minutes in warm water

1½ teaspoons trassi (dried shrimp paste)

1 large onion, finely chopped

4 garlic cloves, finely chopped

1½ teaspoons ground kencur

3 kemiri (candlenuts), roasted (see tip page 106)

1½ teaspoons ground laos (galangal)

1 teaspoon ground turmeric

1. Pound all the bumbu ingredients to a paste using a pestle and mortar.
2. Heat the oil in a wok, add the bumbu paste and fry gently until fragrant, for about 1–2 minutes.
3. Stir in the salam leaves, coconut milk and tamarind puree.
4. Add the fish and mix well. Simmer until the oil floats to the surface and the sauce has thickened. To serve, stir with two forks to flake the fish into the sauce.

Ikan Bumbu Bali
Balinese fish fillets

This famous spicy Balinese sauce tastes delicious with fish. Simmering the fish in the sauce allows it to absorb all the fantastic flavours of turmeric, lemongrass and garlic.

2 tablespoons vegetable oil

2 salam leaves

3 kaffir lime leaves

1½ cm (¾ in) piece fresh laos root (galangal)

½ teaspoon tamarind puree

2 cm (1 in) piece fresh ginger root

300 ml (10½ fl oz / 1¼ cup) water

2 tablespoons kecap manis (sweet soy sauce)

500 g (1 lb 2 oz) firm fish fillets (e.g. mackerel, sole or tilapia), cut into pieces

For the bumbu:

3 garlic cloves

8 shallots, finely chopped

2 lomboks (large red chillies), seeded and finely chopped

½ teaspoon trassi bakar (roasted dried shrimp paste)

4 kemiri (candlenuts), roasted (see tip on page 106)

salt to taste

1. Pound all the bumbu ingredients to a paste using a pestle and mortar.
2. Heat the oil in a wok, add the bumbu paste and fry gently until fragrant, for about 1–2 minutes.
3. Stir in the salam and kaffir lime leaves, the laos, tamarind puree and ginger and cook for a further 1½ minutes.
4. Pour in the water and kecap manis, add the fish and stir gently. Simmer for approx. 10 minutes or until the fish is cooked through. Serve with white rice.

Ikan Kare
mildly spiced fish curry

This is a wonderfully aromatic curry with plenty of flavour. Use any firm type of fish you want.

4 tablespoons vegetable oil

500 g (1 lb 2 oz) red snapper fillet (or any other firm fish), cut into pieces

6 shallots, finely chopped

1 onion, finely chopped

2 garlic cloves, finely chopped

1 lombok (large red chilli), seeded and thinly sliced

1 teaspoon ground ginger

½ teaspoon curry powder

2 teaspoons ground coriander

1 lemongrass stalk, lightly bruised

1 salam leaf

pinch of salt

1 tablespoon tamarind puree, dissolved in 125 ml (4 fl oz / ½ cup) water

250 ml (9 fl oz / 1 cup) coconut milk

1. Heat 2 tablespoons of oil in a wok and carefully brown the fish without cooking it through. Remove the fish from the wok and put aside.
2. Wipe the wok clean with paper towel and return to the heat. Pour in the remaining oil and cook the shallot, onion and garlic until translucent.
3. Add the lombok, ginger, curry powder, coriander, lemongrass, salam leaf and salt. Stir briefly, then add the tamarind water. Simmer for 10 minutes over a low heat.
4. Add the pieces of fish to the sauce, cover and cook for approx. 5 minutes until the fish is just cooked through.
5. Pour in the coconut milk and gently heat through, for about 2 minutes, then serve.

Ikan Balado
fried fish with chilli and shallot bumbu

The word 'balado' is used for dishes served with a spicy red sauce made with lots of chillies and sometimes tomatoes. Examples are terong balado, eggplant in balado sauce, and telur balado, hard-boiled eggs in balado sauce. The sauce is also delicious with fish, as in this recipe, which uses perch or snapper.

½ teaspoon salt

juice of 1 lime

500 g (1 lb 2 oz) firm fish fillet (e.g. perch or snapper)

4 tablespoons vegetable oil

2 kaffir lime leaves

100 ml (3½ fl oz / scant ½ cup) tepid chicken stock

handful celery leaves, coarsely chopped

For the bumbu:

7 shallots, finely chopped

3 garlic cloves, finely chopped

3 cm (1 in) piece fresh laos root (galangal), peeled and finely chopped

5 lomboks (large red chillies), seeded and coarsely chopped

1. Dissolve the salt in the lime juice. Pour over the fish and leave to marinate for approx. 25 minutes.
2. Pat the fish dry. Heat 2 tablespoons of oil in a wok and fry the fish on all sides until golden brown. Remove with a slotted spoon, drain on paper towel and keep warm.
3. Pound all the bumbu ingredients to a paste using a pestle and mortar.
4. Heat the remaining oil in the wok (wipe clean first), add the bumbu paste and fry gently until fragrant, for about 3 minutes.
5. Add the kaffir lime leaves and the stock and simmer for 2 minutes.
6. Place the fish on a serving dish and spoon over the sauce. Scatter with celery leaves and serve.

No Indonesian meal is complete without a good sambal – whether it is a dangerously hot relish made from red hot rawits (Indonesian bird's eye chillies), or a milder, fried variety with tomatoes or fresh sweet gandarias (plum mangos). Even those who do not enjoy spicy food will surely enjoy a small spoonful of fresh sambal to flavour their rice.

Sambal

You can only make the real sambal 'by hand'. Not only does this give juicy chillies and other fresh ingredients a taste that a ready-made sambal cannot compete with, but also through preparation by hand a characteristic smoothness is created. Only by patient, rhythmic crushing of the ulekan (pestle) can you get the perfect sambal texture where all the flavours are released; a machine only crushes and chops the ingredients.

Fortunately, preparing sambal yourself is not difficult; you can prepare a simple sambal ulek within a few minutes.

Chilli for pepper

The spicy lomboks (chillies), which form part of practically every Indonesian meal, are not originally from Asia but from America. Spanish and Portuguese traders brought them to Indonesia from their South American colonies to trade for black and white peppers, which were higly valued in Europe. In Indonesia, chilli quickly became more popular than the indigenous peppers.

Storing sambal

Fresh sambal is best kept in a closed jar in the refrigerator. Depending on the ingredients the sambal will keep for a few days or up to several weeks. (Fried sambal has a longer shelf life than sambal made from fresh chillies.) Smooth the top of the sambal and pour a layer of (arachis) oil on it so that oxygen can not reach it. You can freeze (non-fresh) sambal in portions; it will last for months without really losing its flavour.

Sambal Ulek
the basic sambal

Sambal ulek can be considered the basic sambal. It's named after the ulekan, the typical Indonesian pestle that belongs to the cobek, the Indonesian mortar.

20 lomboks (large red chillies)
2 teaspoons salt

1. Slit the lomboks open lengthwise. Leave the seeds in if you want it very hot, or rinse them out if not. Finely chop the flesh.
2. Using a pestle and mortar, pound the lombok and salt together until smooth.

Tip: Sambal ulek lasts very well in a sealed jar in the refrigerator.

Sambal Kering Ebi
shrimp and shallot sambal

8 shallots, thinly sliced
200 g (7 oz) finely chopped seeded lomboks (large chillies)
3 tablespoons vegetable oil
sea salt to taste
200 g (7 oz) ebi (dried shrimps), soaked for 30 minutes in
   tepid water then drained
juice of ½ lemon

1. Fry the shallot and lombok gently in the oil until
   translucent, for about 2 minutes. Add salt to taste and
   reduce the heat to very low. Leave to simmer until
   everything is very soft.
2. Stir in the ebi and lemon juice and cook for at least
   10 minutes longer. Transfer to small bowls and allow
   to cool.

Sambal Goreng Lombok Hijau
green sambal

200 g (7 oz) finely chopped seeded green lomboks
   (large chillies)
2 tablespoons tepid water
8 shallots, thinly sliced
50 ml (2 fl oz) vegetable oil
salt to taste
2 green tomatoes, diced
1 x 50 g (1¾ oz) can anchovy fillets, finely chopped

1. Mix the lombok with the tepid water.
2. Fry the shallots in 2 tablespoons of oil until golden. Add
   the lombok and salt, stir then cook until soft, for about
   2 minutes.
3. Stir in the tomato, anchovy and the remaining oil and
   simmer for 15 minutes. Allow to cool before serving.

Sambal Lada Udang Kering
dried shrimp and coconut sambal

4 shallots, finely chopped
15 lomboks (large red chillies), seeded and finely chopped
pinch of sea salt
100 ml (3½ fl oz / scant ½ cup) vegetable oil
100 g (4 oz) ebi (dried shrimps), soaked in tepid water,
   then drained and finely chopped
100 ml (3½ fl oz / scant ½ cup) coconut milk or
   coconut cream
juice of ½ lemon

1. Pound the shallot and lombok with a little salt, using a
   pestle and mortar.
2. Gently fry the lombok mixture in half of the oil until very
   soft.
3. Add the ebi and mix well.
4. Pour in the coconut milk (or coconut cream) and cook,
   uncovered, for about 10 minutes over a medium heat. For
   a richer sambal, you can stir in the remaining oil.
5. Remove the sambal from the heat and add the lemon
   juice. Allow to cool.

Sambal Trassi
red onion and shrimp paste sambal

10 lomboks (large red chillies), seeded and finely chopped
1 small red onion, finely chopped
1 tablespoon trassi (dried shrimp paste)
a little sea salt
juice of ½ lemon

1. Pound all ingredients, except the lemon juice, using a pestle
   and mortar.
2. Stir in enough lemon juice to make a smooth sambal. Keep
   in a tightly sealed jar in the refrigerator.

Sambal: explosions of colour, aroma and flavour

In a market in Indonesia, between the baskets of shiny chillies and stalls with fresh herbs that you can only dream of, they are displayed in trays: dozens of sambal varieties, from mild green to red hot 'Satan's sambal' and deep reddish-brown fried sambal. The air is filled with the smell of sweet browned shallots that have been fried in oil mixed with the penetrating shrimp pastes and tingling of juicy fresh chillies.

Combining the right sambal with the right dish is one of the most important 'arts' of Indonesian cuisine. Not every sambal combines well with every dish. The simplest sambal is a thick sauce of red or green chillies, finely crushed with salt. It is served separately, so that everyone can add as much as they want. In addition, sambal is the basis of many Indonesian dishes such as sambal goreng ati (chicken livers in a spicy sauce) and sambal goreng udang (prawns in sambal and coconut milk). There are more reasons than just the spicy flavour for why Indonesians are fond of hot chilli sauce. Sambal is, for example, good for the appetite, it is used to purify the tastebuds and help the digestion. Moreover, the extra chilli heat, particularly in a tropical climate, is very pleasant: it stimulates the sweat glands and accelerates the blood circulation. You get warmer for a little while, and then your body can actually tolerate the heat better.

Addictive

The substance that makes chillies spicy is called capsaicin. There are several types of this substance, which explains why some chillies immediately give a hot sensation in the mouth that quickly disappears, while others produce a heat which begins slowly and continues for longer. The more capsaicin you eat, the more your body gets used to it and the more you can eat before you get the same burning sensation. The 'pain' in your mouth makes your body create endorphins, which in turn ensures a feeling of happiness – eating a lot of sambal can actually make you a bit high. According to some, this is why some people become so fond of spicy chillies. The hotter, the better …

Sambal Gandaria
gandaria fruit sambal

1 tablespoon ebi (dried shrimps), soaked in tepid water
  then drained and chopped
6 gandaria fruits (plum mangos), finely chopped
½ teaspoon trassi (dried shrimp paste)
5 lomboks (large red chillies), seeded and finely chopped
pinch of sea salt
1 tablespoon vegetable oil (or 1 tablespoon tepid water)

1. Using a pestle and mortar, pound all ingredients, except
   the oil, to a paste (or you may want to use a food processor for this sambal).
2. Stir in enough oil (or tepid water) to obtain a smooth
   mixture.

Sambal Kecap
salty kecap sambal

50 ml (2 fl oz) kecap asin or Chinese soy sauce
2 lomboks (large red chillies), seeded and sliced into rings
4 shallots, thinly sliced
juice of ½ lemon

1. Using a pestle and mortar, pound all ingredients, except
   the lemon juice, to a paste.
2. Stir in enough lemon juice to obtain a smooth mixture.
   Keep in a tightly sealed jar in the refrigerator.

Tip: Raw chillies are more easily chopped if they are
heated in a dry saucepan beforehand. To prevent
discolouring, keep swirling the chillies around. Cut
them roughly, remove the seeds if necessary and then
grind them up using the pestle and mortar.

Sambal Lada Uap
steamed peasant-style sambal

5 lomboks (large red chillies), seeded and finely chopped
½ red onion, finely chopped
1 teaspoon trassi (dried shrimp paste), briefly dry-fried
  then crumbled
2 firm tomatoes, seeded and finely chopped
sea salt to taste

1. Steam the lombok and the red onion until completely
   soft (either in a steamer or in a colander placed over a
   pan of boiling water). This will take approx. 8 minutes.
2. Pound the mixture in a pestle and mortar (or food
   processor), then mix in the trassi, tomato and salt.

Sambal Bajak
hot and sweet sambal with candlenuts and shallots

You'll find this sambal often as a table condiment
for seasoning noodles, rice, soups and other
dishes.

5 shallots, finely chopped
1 garlic clove, finely chopped
10 lomboks (large red chillies), seeded and finely chopped
3 tablespoons vegetable oil
1 salam leaf
2½ cm (1 in) piece fresh laos root (galangal)
pinch of sea salt
2 teaspoons gula jawa (palm sugar)
10 kemiri (candlenuts), roasted (see tip on page 106),
  then finely pounded

1. Using a pestle and mortar, pound the shallot, garlic and
   lombok to a coarse paste.
2. Fry the lombok mixture gently in the oil until completely
   tender. Add the remaining ingredients and simmer for
   at least 10 minutes longer over a low heat. Transfer to a
   bowl and leave to cool.

Sambal Soto Ayam
sambal for chicken soup

5 lomboks (large red chillies), seeded and finely chopped
5 rawits (bird's eye chillies), finely chopped
5 kemiri (candlenuts), roasted (see tip on page 106), then finely pounded
½ teaspoon trassi bakar (roasted dried shrimp paste)
2 tablespoons lemon juice
sea salt
kecap manis (sweet soy sauce, optional)

1. Gently fry the lombok and rawit with the kemiri and trassi bakar until the chillies are completely soft.
2. Remove from the heat and stir in the lemon juice. Season with sea salt and kecap manis, if using.

Sambal Tomat
oven-roasted tomato sambal

300 g (10½ oz) ripe tomatoes, skinned and coarsely chopped
3 lomboks (large red chillies), seeded and finely chopped
3 rawits (bird's eye chillies), finely chopped
½ teaspoon trassi (dried shrimp paste), finely pounded
juice of ½ lemon

1. Preheat the oven to 225°C (425°F / Gas 7).
2. Place the tomato, lombok and rawit in an ovenproof dish. Roast in the oven for about 25 minutes or until softened.
3. Add the trassi, stir well then pound to a smooth sambal using a pestle and mortar. Season to taste with lemon juice.

Sambal Ketupat Betawi
traditional dry-fried Javanese sambal

1 tablespoon vegetable oil
5 lomboks (large red chillies), seeded and finely chopped
½ red onion, finely chopped
½ teaspoon trassi (dried shrimp paste)
3 kemiri (candlenuts), roasted (see tip on page 106), then finely pounded
50 g (1¾ oz) ebi (dried shrimps), soaked in tepid water then finely pounded
½ teaspoon ground laos (galangal)

1. In the oil gently fry the lombok and onion for about 1 minute, then add the trassi and kemiri and cook until completely soft.
2. Stir in the ebi and laos and gently fry until dry.

Sambal Tempeh
spicy tempeh sambal

5 lomboks (large red chillies), seeded and finely chopped
5 rawits (bird's eye chillies), finely chopped
150 g (5½ oz) piece of tempeh, chopped and fried in vegetable oil until golden
½ teaspoon trassi (dried shrimp paste)
1 tablespoon kecap manis (sweet soy sauce)
sea salt to taste
2 tablespoons vegetable oil
1 tablespoon lemon juice

1. Mix all ingredients, except the oil and the lemon juice, together.
2. Heat the oil, add the chilli mixture and cook until fragrant and soft.
3. Season with lemon juice and allow to cool completely.

A matter of taste

Try and experiment by preparing different textures. Some people love a coarser sambal, while others prefer to crush it for longer to create an almost a smooth paste. Some fried sambals are not crushed finely: paper thin slices of shallot and garlic are crispy fried in hot oil then mixed with trassi and finely chopped chillies.

The delights that you buy anywhere on the streets in Indonesia are often hard to find here. Fortunately you can also make them yourself at home. Try crispy spring rolls with chicken, prawns and bean sprouts as a starter or spicy rujak with sweet and sour fruit for lunch. Or eat them just as they were meant to be eaten,

Snacks and sweets

as a tasty (and in many cases healthy!) snack between meals.

Sweet dishes in Indonesia are not only for after the main meal: sweet pudding, jelly and biscuits of sticky rice and coconut, are snacked on all day. Ice cream and cold drinks are deliciously refreshing during a long hot afternoon. Fresh fruit is often eaten after a meal, which is good for the digestion. After dinner, there is normally something sweet with the coffee such as a piece of *spekkoek* or lapis legit, literally 'sweet, sticky layers' – a beautiful cake which is baked layer by layer.

Bakpao
meat-filled steamed buns

Soft, homemade bakpaos are utterly irresistible and they're easier to prepare than you might expect.

For the dough:

25 g (1 oz) fresh yeast (or 7 g / 1 sachet dried yeast)

150 ml (5 fl oz / ⅔ cup) tepid milk

500 g (1 lb 2 oz / 4 cups) plain flour

1 tablespoon butter

1 tablespoon sugar

1 large egg

pinch of salt

baking paper, cut into 7 cm (2½ in) squares

For the filling:

1 onion, finely chopped

5 garlic cloves, finely chopped

1 tablespoon butter

1 tablespoon finely chopped leek or spring onion

1 tablespoon finely chopped celery leaves (optional)

150 g (5½ oz) minced pork

3–4 tablespoons kecap asin or Chinese soy sauce

1 tablespoon sugar

salt and pepper

1. For the filling, gently fry the onion and garlic in the butter until softened. Mix in the remaining filling ingredients and simmer over a low heat until the pork is cooked through. Remove from the heat and allow to cool before placing in the refrigerator (the mixture is ready when it's well cooled and very firm).

2. Make the dough by stirring the yeast into the milk. Gradually add the flour and mix in the butter, sugar, egg and salt. Knead to a smooth dough then roll into a sausage shape with 10 cm (4 in) diameter. Cut the roll into 2 cm (1 in) discs.

3. Place approx. 1 tablespoon of the filling in the centre of each dough disc. Fold the dough over the filling, pinching the edges together to seal them.

4. Place each bakpao on a square of baking parchment, cover and allow to rise in a warm place for 1 hour. The dough should be springy to the touch when ready.

5. Put the buns in a steamer (it will require several batches to steam them all) and steam, covered, for approx. 10 minutes. If you have no steamer, steam the buns for 10 minutes in a (steamer) basket over a wok or saucepan of simmering water, covered with a lid wrapped in a tea towel to catch the steam.

Risoles
savoury pancake snacks

Risoles are another example of tasty 'Indisch' (from the former Dutch East Indies) food. Thin pancakes are filled with a creamy mixture, folded into parcels and deep-fried until golden, not unlike spring rolls. The contents of the filling can vary but chicken is usually one of the main ingredients. Serve the risoles with a spicy chilli sauce.

1 tablespoon vegetable oil + oil for deep-frying

1 onion, finely chopped

250 g (9 oz) minced chicken/pork/beef, or chicken meat, diced

1 heaped tablespoon finely chopped young leek or spring onion

1 heaped tablespoon finely chopped celery leaves

1 heaped tablespoon finely chopped carrot

1 heaped tablespoon green peas

salt and sugar to taste

1 tablespoon flour

dash of milk

freshly ground black pepper

pinch of grated nutmeg

1 tablespoon butter, at room temperature

1 egg yolk, beaten

dried breadcrumbs

For the pancakes:

100 g (3½ oz) plain flour

pinch of salt

3 eggs, beaten

400 ml (14 fl oz / 1⅝ cups) water

butter for frying

1. To make the pancake batter, sieve the flour and salt into a bowl. Stir in the egg and 100 ml (3½ fl oz / scant ½ cup) of water and mix well. Gradually add enough of the remaining water, stirring all the time, to give a smooth pancake batter. Cover and leave to rest in a cool place for 30 minutes.

2. Meanwhile, make the filling: heat 1 tablespoon of oil in a wok, add the onion, minced or diced (chicken) meat, leek, celery leaves, carrot and peas and stir-fry over a medium heat until the meat is cooked through. Add salt and sugar to taste.

3. In a bowl, whisk the flour, milk, pepper, nutmeg and butter until smooth. Stir into the filling mixture and continue to stir and cook until the filling has thickened. Remove from the heat and allow to cool completely.

4. Meanwhile, cook the pancakes by melting a little butter in a small (20 cm / 8 in diameter) non-stick frying pan. Ladle some batter into the hot pan, swirling evenly to spread. Gently fry for 1–2 minutes each side, tossing to turn. Repeat with the remaining batter.

5. Fill the pancakes with the meat mixture and fold into quarters. Dip in the egg yolk, roll carefully in breadcrumbs and deep-fry in hot oil until golden brown and crisp. Drain on paper towel and serve.

Tropical fruit for savoury and sweet food

You will always find an abundance of beautiful, sweet-smelling exotic fruit in all shapes and sizes and bright colours at Indonesian markets. Indonesians love them: they eat fruit as a snack, dessert, prepared in sweet dishes and even in savoury dishes such as rujak (a salad of, for example, pineapple, mango, cucumber and grapefruit with a spicy sauce) or sayur asem (a sour soup with unripe nangka 'jackfruit' and sour star fruit).

Belimbing (carambola, star fruit)
Belimbing looks beautiful when cut into slices and the juicy star slices are lovely in a fruit salad. Young belimbing is sugar coated and eaten as a sweet.

Delima (pomegranate)
Delima is a pomegranate and the fresh, sweet and very healthy seeds are delicious on, for example, ice cream. Bidji delima, literally 'pomegranate seeds', is also a dish made from tapioca pearls.

Durians
Durians are notorious for their strong smell. Inside the prickly skin they contain large pieces of creamy flesh, each surrounding a stone. Among other things they are used to make a sauce that you eat with a sweetened porridge of sticky rice and coconut.

Gandaria (plum mango)
Gandaria is a smaller relative of the mango with soft, juicy flesh. Its sweet and sour taste is a refreshing ingredient in some sambals.

Jeruk besar, jeruk bali (grapefruit and pomelo)
Jeruk besar and jeruk bali are slightly bitter citrus fruits – the pomelo (bali) is larger than a grapefruit (besar) and tastes a little sweeter. The juicy flesh is very thirst quenching. These fruits are also used in rujak.

Kelengkeng (longan)
Kelengkengs, ramboetans and lychees are all related. These refreshing small fruits are delicious as a snack in hot weather. A jelly can be made from sweet syrup flavoured with kelengkeng juice, which you can eat as a dessert or a snack.

Manggis (Mangos)
Manggis have a delicious, pungent, sweet and aromatic flesh and it can be eaten out of your hand or prepared in drinks or ice cream. Unripe mangos are also used in savoury dishes such as sambal mangga and acar mangga.

Nangka ('jackfruit')
Nangka looks like a breadfruit, but contains less starch. Various dishes are made from it, anything from ice cream to chips and Javanese gudeg, which is young boiled nangka with palm sugar, coconut, garlic and spices.

Pepaya (papaya)
Pepaya has a green skin and juicy reddish-orange flesh with small black seeds. The fruit is often eaten as a dessert as it is good for the digestion.

Pisang (banana)
There are many different kinds of pisang, from sweet little bananas as big as a thumb to the larger, familiar kind. The pisang tanduk is a plantain, a banana type suitable for frying, for example, in an airy fried dough jacket as pisang goreng.

Lumpia
fried spring rolls

1 onion, finely chopped

3 garlic cloves, finely chopped

vegetable oil

150 g (5½ oz) boneless pork, diced (or use minced pork)

150 g (5½ oz) cooked shrimps

2 tablespoons finely chopped boneless chicken meat

3 thin slices ham, finely chopped

1 tablespoon finely chopped leek

1 tablespoon finely chopped celery leaves

100 g (3½ oz) white cabbage, shredded

150 g (5½ oz) bean sprouts

salt and pepper

egg yolk (or water and flour), to seal lumpia wrapper edges

4 ready-made lumpia (spring roll) wrappers,
  thawed if frozen

1. Using a pestle and mortar, pound the onion and garlic to a paste. Fry the paste in a little oil until softened.

2. Add the pork, shrimps, chicken, ham, vegetables and salt and pepper and stir-fry until the meat is cooked through and the mixture is dry. Remove from the heat and allow to cool.

3. Divide the mixture between the lumpia wrappers and fold three corners into the centre to cover the filling. Fold up towards the remaining corner then seal the edges with egg yolk or a mixture of water and flour.

4. Deep-fry the lumpias (in 2 batches) in plenty of hot oil until golden brown. Beware: overfilling the rolls or not using enough oil will cause the rolls to burst. Drain on paper towel then serve immediately.

Pangsit Goreng
wontons with chilli and ginger dip

200 g (7 oz) mince (mixture of minced pork and prawns or minced pork and beef)

8 garlic cloves, finely chopped

2 spring onions, finely chopped

1 tablespoon finely chopped celery leaves

salt and pepper

24 ready-made wonton wrappers (or 6 spring roll wrappers, quartered)

water and flour, to seal the wonton edges

vegetable oil for deep-frying

For the chilli and ginger dip:

1 x 70 g (2½ oz) small can tomato puree

200 ml (7 fl oz / 1 scant cup) water

2 teaspoons ground ginger

2 cm (1 in) piece fresh ginger root

1 teaspoon Sambal Ulek (see page 238)

2 teaspoons sugar

pinch of salt

50 ml (2 fl oz) rice vinegar

50 ml (2 fl oz) stem ginger syrup (optional)

2 teaspoons cornflour

1. Make the dip by placing the tomato puree and water into a saucepan. Stir in the ground ginger, ginger root, sambal, sugar and salt and slowly bring to the boil, stirring all the time. Reduce the heat and continue to stir for 1 minute, then add the vinegar and ginger syrup (if using).

2. Thicken the dip with a little cornflour, remove from the heat and allow to cool completely. Discard the piece of ginger just before serving.

3. Mix the mince with the garlic, spring onion and celery leaves. Add salt and pepper to taste.

4. Place teaspoonfuls of filling in the centre of each wrapper. Brush the edges with some water and flour mixture.

5. Fold the wrappers diagonally in half to enclose the filling and form a triangle. Pull the top and bottom corners up to meet each other, so that one corner overlaps the other slightly. Press the ends together to seal.

6. Deep-fry in hot oil until golden brown and crisp. Drain on paper towel and serve with the dip alongside.

Lumpia

Semarang, the capital of west Java, is famous for its lumpias (a type of spring roll). The original lumpia semarang recipe was introduced by Chinese immigrants. Lumpia has many forms and variations and is not always deep-fried: 'wet' lumpias (lumpia basah) are lumpia wrappers that are rolled around a filling and served immediately.

Pangsit Goreng

These thin, crispy fried wontons stuffed with spiced-up minced meat are divine. The stuffing can vary but a mixture of minced pork and prawns is a firm favourite. Pangsit (or wonton) wrappers are available from Asian food shops.

Pastel Goreng
mini-fried meat pies

Indonesians love savoury snacks like lumpias, wontons and risoles and these tasty little half-moon shaped pies. The filling is so tasty that the pies don't need a dip, but serve a small bowl of spicy chilli sauce alongside if you wish.

For the pastry:

500 g (1 lb 2 oz / 4 cups) flour
250 ml (9 oz / 1 cup) coconut cream
1 egg
pinch of salt
knob of butter
water and flour, to seal the edges
vegetable oil for deep-frying

For the filling:

½ onion, finely chopped
2 garlic cloves, finely chopped
4 kemiri (candlenuts), roasted (see tip on page 106)
1 tablespoon ground coriander
1 teaspoon ground cumin
½ teaspoon ground turmeric
1 teaspoon trassi (dried shrimp paste)
pinch each of salt and sugar
2 tablespoons vegetable oil
2 cm (1 in) piece fresh laos root (galangal)
2 salam leaves
125 g (4½ oz) minced pork
125 g (4½ oz) minced beef
150 ml (5 fl oz) coconut cream

1. For the filling, use a pestle and mortar to pound together the onion, garlic, kemiri, coriander, cumin, turmeric, trassi, salt and a little sugar to form a smooth paste. Heat a little oil in a wok, add the paste and fry gently until fragrant. Stir in the laos and the salam leaves.

2. Add the meat and continue to stir-fry until it is cooked through. Pour in the coconut cream and stir until the mixture is completely dry. Remove from the heat and allow to cool.

3. For the pastry, knead the flour, coconut cream, egg, salt and enough butter to form a compact pastry that does not stick to the hand. Add a little extra coconut cream if necessary it. Roll out into a thin rectangle and cut out pastry circles.

4. Divide the filling mixture (discard the laos and salam leaves first) into the middle of the pastry circles and fold the pastry in half into half-moon shapes, pinching out the air and sealing the edges with a little water and flour mixture. Use a fork to press the edges.

5. Deep-fry the pies in batches until golden brown and crisp in hot oil. Drain on paper towel and serve.

Lemper Ayam
sticky rice rolls with chicken

Javanese lempers are stuffed sticky rice rolls. The filling usually contains a spiced-up minced chicken mixture. They can be served warm or cold.

250 g (9 oz) glutinous rice (ketan), rinsed and drained

400 ml (14 fl oz / 1⅔ cups) water

50 g (1¾ oz) creamed coconut, crumbled

salt

2 tablespoons vegetable oil

225 g (8 oz) minced chicken

2 salam leaves

1 kaffir lime leaf

freshly ground black pepper

squeeze of lemon juice

For the bumbu:

3 shallots, finely chopped

2 garlic cloves, finely chopped

2 teaspoons ground coriander

1 teaspoon ground cumin

½ teaspoon ground turmeric

½ teaspoon trassi (dried shrimp paste)

1 teaspoon gula jawa (palm sugar), crushed

1. Place the glutinous rice in a pan and add the water. Bring to the boil, reduce the heat and simmer for 15 minutes.

2. Add half of the creamed coconut and a pinch of salt and continue to cook over a low heat until the rice is tender, for about 10 minutes.

3. Spread the hot rice onto a platter or baking tray and allow to cool.

4. Using a pestle and mortar, pound all the bumbu ingredients to a smooth paste. Gently fry the bumbu in the oil until fragrant. Add the chicken, salam and kaffir lime leaves, then stir in the remaining creamed coconut and a dash of water. Stir-fry until the chicken is cooked through and the mixture is dry. Season with salt, pepper and a squeeze of lemon juice. Remove from the heat and allow to cool. Discard the salam and kaffir lime leaves.

5. Brush sheets of plastic wrap with oil. Spoon heaped tablespoonfuls of sticky rice onto the plastic wrap sheets and shape into rectangles 1 cm (¼–½ in) thick. Spread some filling along the centre of each rice rectangle from end to end, then fold both sides of the wrap towards each other lengthwise. Shape into firm rolls between your hands. Twist the ends of the wrap together to seal.

6. To serve the lempers, reheat in their plastic wrapping in a steamer (or microwave oven) and serve warm or at room temperature.

Pandan Sponge Cake

Be warned: this wonderfully light and airy green sponge cake is extremely moreish. Make sure all ingredients are at room temperature before you start. The pandan essence is not only used to colour (it is 100 percent natural colouring), but also to flavour the cake. Beware of cheap, artificial essences containing chemical additives and artificial colouring agents.

5 eggs
250 g (9 oz) caster sugar
a few drops of pandan essence
250 g (9 oz / 2 cups) flour, sieved
50 g (1¾ oz) cornflour, sieved
pinch of salt
1 teaspoon finely grated lemon zest
icing sugar (optional)

1. Preheat the oven to 180°C (355°F / Gas 4). Prepare a 23-cm (9-in) round cake tin by greasing then dusting with flour.
2. Place the eggs and sugar in a heatproof mixing bowl over a large saucepan of simmering water (make sure the water does not touch the bowl) and whisk briskly with an electric mixer until the mixture thickens and almost doubles in volume, for about 8 minutes.
3. Remove from the heat and whisk in the pandan essence. Continue to whisk until the mixture cools.
4. Gradually fold in the flour, cornflour, salt and lemon zest using a spatula.
5. Pour the mixture into the prepared cake tin, place just below the middle of the oven and bake for approx. 1 hour or until springy to the touch.
6. Remove the cake from the oven and allow to cool slightly before turning it out onto a wire rack to cool. Sprinkle with icing sugar if desired.

Onde-onde
sesame balls filled with sweet bean paste

There is sometimes a little confusion between onde-onde and klepon (green, sweet sticky rice balls stuffed with palm sugar, see page 268) because in Malaysia klepon are called 'onde-onde'. Genuine Indonesian onde-onde or onde-onde ketawa ('Javanese style') are addictive sticky rice balls with a sweet mung bean filling and a sesame seed crust.

300 g (10½ oz) kacang hijau (mung beans), soaked overnight in plenty of water
salt
160 g (5¾ oz) gula jawa (palm sugar)
2 thin strips fresh or frozen pandan leaf
100 ml (3½ oz / scant ½ cup) coconut cream
a little flour or tapioca starch for thickening
500 g (1 lb 2 oz / 5 cups) glutinous rice flour
150 ml (5 fl oz) coconut milk
handful of sesame seeds
vegetable oil for deep-frying

1. For the filling, cook the drained mung beans with salt in enough fresh water to cover. Once the beans are soft, add the palm sugar and pandan leaf. Cook, stirring, over a very low heat until well combined.
2. Add the coconut cream and thicken with a little flour or starch until the mixture can be shaped.
3. Knead the rice flour with some salt and the coconut milk to form a dough. Shape into balls just a little larger than a golf ball.
4. Flatten the balls and place some sweet bean filling in the centre. Close the dough around the filling and reshape into balls.
5. Dip the balls quickly into water to dampen the surface then roll them in sesame seeds. Deep-fry the balls in hot oil in batches until golden brown. Drain on paper towel.

Kue Lapis
layered coconut cake

Kue (or 'kwee') lapis, with its mysterious layered structure, is not as difficult to make as it looks. The cake tastes delicious with Sumatran coffee, which is regarded as the best in the country.

180 g (6 oz / scant 2 cups) glutinous rice flour

180 g (6 oz) tapioca

400 g (14 oz) sugar

pinch of salt

900 ml (31½ fl oz) coconut milk

5 sachets (40 g) vanilla sugar

a few drops of pink food colouring

1. Line a 22-cm (8½-in) springfrom cake tin with foil.
2. Mix all the ingredients, except the food colouring, to a batter and divide into 2.
3. Dye 1 part with a few drops of pink food colouring.
4. Preheat a steamer and wrap the lid with a clean tea towel to capture the steam.
5. Spoon a thin layer of uncoloured batter into the spring-form tin. Steam for approx. 5 minutes until it sets and looks shiny. Add a thin layer of pink-coloured batter to the tin and steam again.
6. Continue the process alternately until all the batter is used up. The whole process may take up to 3 hours. The final layers may have to steam longer, for about 10 minutes each.
7. Allow to cool completely before cutting into thin slices.

Klepon
sticky rice dumplings with melted palm sugar

Everybody loves these little dumplings made of sticky rice with melted palm sugar oozing out of them. Klepon tastes and looks wonderfully exotic due to the pandan essence, which also gives the dumplings their gorgeous aroma. Only add a few drops of the essence though, as it's easily overdone.

200 g (7 oz / 2 cups) glutinous rice flour

pinch of salt

6 drops pandan essence

150 ml (5 fl oz / ⅔ cup) water

100 g (3½ oz) gula jawa (palm sugar), broken into pieces

75 g (2½ oz) desiccated coconut

2 tablespoons tepid water

1. Mix the rice flour, salt and pandan essence. Gradually knead in enough water to form a firm dough.
2. Shape the dough into little balls (slightly smaller than a golf ball) and push a piece of palm sugar into the middle of each ball, making sure that the dough completely surrounds the sugar on all sides.
3. Spread the coconut on a plate and sprinkle with the tepid water. Set aside.
4. Cook the balls in simmering water in a wok or large saucepan until they float to the surface.
5. Remove the balls from the water using two spoons (they are extremely sticky) and roll them immediately in the coconut. Allow to cool on baking paper.

'Stinky fruit'

'It smells like hell and tastes like heaven' is what the Indonesians say about durians. This strange fruit with its prickly exterior has farinaceous, sweet flesh that many Asians are crazy about – it tastes creamy and a little like custard, vanilla and caramel, but with a hint of onion and cheese. Once you cut the skin open, a very pungent smell spreads: durians smell so bad that it is forbidden to eat them in public places such as trains or hotels!

Pisang Goreng
banana fritters

These sweet and crispy fritters are served as a side dish or snack. Ripe plantains are a variety of banana that cannot be eaten raw but, once cooked, are deliciously sweet. Unripe plantains however, are very starchy and usually served as a vegetable. When ripe, the skin of a plantain will be mostly brown or black and the flesh will be soft, retaining its firm shape when cooked.

125 g (4½ oz / 1 cup) self-raising flour
2 tablespoons glutinous rice flour
1 egg white (optional)
pinch of salt
water
3 ripe pisang tanduk (horn plantain)
vegetable oil for deep-frying
icing sugar (optional)

1. Place the self-raising flour, rice flour, egg white (if using) and salt in a bowl and add enough water to make a smooth batter, similar to pancake batter.
2. Peel the plantains, halve them lengthwise and cut each half into equal pieces.
3. Dip the plantain pieces into the batter to coat, then deep-fry in batches in hot oil until golden brown and crisp. Drain on paper towel and sprinkle with icing sugar if desired.

Rempeyek Kacang
crispy peanut wafers

The batter for these wafers should be perfectly smooth and quite thin, but not too thin or else the wafers will fall apart during cooking. Serve the rempeyek as a snack or as part of an elaborate rice table.

110 g (4 oz / 1 scant cup) rice flour (or plain flour)
1 tablespoon cornflour
120 ml (3½ fl oz / ½ cup) coconut milk
1 tablespoon ground almonds
2 garlic cloves, crushed
1 small onion, grated
1 teaspoon ground coriander
50 g (1¾ oz) kacang tanah (raw peanuts, or use ordinary
  unsalted peanuts)
salt and pepper
vegetable oil

1. Sieve the rice flour and cornflour into a bowl. Gradually mix in enough coconut milk to make a smooth batter.
2. In another bowl, mix together the almond with the garlic, onion and coriander. Add to the batter, along with the peanuts and a little salt and pepper.
3. Heat a layer of oil for deep-frying in a wok. Meanwhile, heat 1 tablespoon of oil in a non-stick frying pan. Ladle tablespoons of the batter into the frying pan, smoothing them out with the back of the tablespoon until they form separate flat shapes (cook no more than 3–4 at a time). Once the wafers come loose, transfer them to the wok immediately and deep-fry until crisp and golden. Drain on paper towel and allow to cool. Continue until the batter is used up.

Lapis Legit
layered spice cake

Lapis legit (also known as 'kue lapis') is arguably the best known Indonesian cake. The cake is firm yet tender, very aromatic and a little moist. Preparing it requires time because you need to bake each layer separately – it consists of up to 40 layers! – however, many people find this quite therapeutic.

10 eggs, separated
250 g (9 oz) icing sugar
400 g (14½ oz) butter, melted
250 g (9 oz) flour, sieved
2 teaspoons ground cinnamon
1 teaspoon ground cloves
1 teaspoon ground cardamom
½–1 teaspoon ground nutmeg

1. Cream the egg yolks and sugar together with a whisk. Add 250 g of the melted butter and beat well. Fold in the flour and spices using a spatula.
2. Beat the egg whites until stiff, then fold into the yolk mixture.
3. Preheat a grill oven to 170°C (335°F / Gas 3). Once the oven is hot, switch it to its medium grill function. Grease a 22-cm (8½-in) springform cake tin.
4. Pour a thin layer of the batter into the prepared tin. Spread it out evenly and bake until golden brown, for about 3–4 minutes.
5. Remove the tin from the oven and brush the layer of cake with some melted butter.
6. Pour in another thin layer of batter on top of the cake and bake again until golden brown and done, then brush with butter. Continue the process until all the batter has been used up.
7. Allow the cake to cool completely in the tin before cutting into thin slices.

Rujak
spicy fruit salad

Most Indonesians, pregnant women in particular, love the combination of sweet, sour, salty and spicy flavours in rujak salad. Authentic rujak uses green mangos to enhance the sweet and sour tang. This recipe contains various exotic fruits for a slightly sweeter favour.

1 pepaya (papaya), peeled, seeded and cubed
100 g (3½ oz) lychees, peeled and stone removed
½ pineapple, peeled and cubed
1 mango, peeled, pitted and cut into pieces

For the dressing:
2 teaspoons Sambal Ulek (see page 238) or Sambal Trassi (see page 240)
3 tablespoons gula jawa (palm sugar), crushed
2 tablespoons kecap manis (sweet soy sauce)
1 tablespoon lemon juice
2 tablespoons water

1. Combine all the dressing ingredients.
2. Toss the dressing with the fruit or serve the fruit with the dressing alongside.

Kue Mangkuk
coconut cupcakes

These little steamed cakes have a gorgeous, delicate taste. If you don't have proper cupcake moulds use coffee cups or small bowls instead. Place them in a bamboo steamer basket (available from Asian food shops) over a wok filled with a layer of simmering water, making sure the water does not touch the bottom of the basket. The cupcakes are ready when they're dry on top and starting to burst open.

500 g (2 lb 2 oz / 4 cups) self-raising flour
2 sachets (16 g) vanilla sugar
140 g (5 oz) desiccated coconut + extra to garnish
  (optional)
600 ml (20 fl oz / 2½ cup) sparkling mineral water
pinch of salt
280 g (10 oz) caster sugar
a few drops of pink food colouring
a few drops of pandan essence

1. Combine all ingredients, except the food colouring and pandan essence, in a mixing bowl. Divide the mixture in half, and add pink food colouring to one part and the pandan essence to the other.
2. Rinse small heatproof cups with cold water then fill them up to four-fifths full with the mixture.
3. Preheat a steamer (or hang a steamer basket over a wok or pan of simmering water).
4. Steam the cupcakes, covered, for approx. 30 minutes or until the cakes open up.
5. Garnish with grated coconut if desired.

Roti Kukus
steamed sponge cake

The soft texture of this airy sponge cake is incredible. And there's not a gram of fat in sight. For an even lighter result add an egg-cup of sparkling mineral water or lemonade to the batter.

5 eggs
300 g (10½ oz) sugar
1 sachet (8 g) vanilla sugar
200 g (7 oz / 1½ cups) self-raising flour, sieved

1. Cream the eggs, sugar and vanilla sugar using a food processor.
2. Gradually add the flour and beat until combined.
3. Preheat a steamer (or hang a steamer basket over a wok or saucepan of simmering water).
4. Place a tea towel into the steamer basket then line with baking paper. Also wrap the steamer's lid with a tea towel to catch the steam.
5. Pour the batter into the prepared steamer basket and steam, covered, for approx. 1 hour or until dry on top. Do not remove the steamer's lid during the steaming process. The cake may or may not burst during steaming.
6. Allow to cool before slicing and serving.

Glossary

See 'Basic Ingredients of Indonesian Cuisine' (pages 34–53) for more detailed information on specific ingredients.

A

acar: pickles

acar manis: sweet and sour

agar-agar: a gelatine type of seaweed

asem: tamarind

asin: salty, salted

ati: liver

ayam: chicken

B

babi: pork

bakmi: Chinese noodles

balado: with chillies

bawang: onion

bawang merah: red onion or shallot

bawang putih: garlic

bebek: duck (Javanese)

belimbing: carambola or star fruit

beras: peeled, uncooked rice

beras hitam: black rice

beras ketan: glutinous rice

beras menir: broken rice

beras merah: red rice

bihun: rice vermicelli noodles

biji: pits or seeds

brambang: red shallot

brem: rice wine

buah: fruit (general)

bubur: rice porridge (sweet or savoury)

bumbu: spice mixture

buncis: green beans

C

cabe: chilli

cabe hijau: green chilli

cabe merah: red chilli

cendol: sweet drink with syrup, coconut and grated ice

cengkeh: cloves

cobek: Indonesian mortar

cuka: vinegar

cumi: squid

cumis: fried in oil and stewed, frying

D

dadar: omelette

daging: meat

daging kambing: goat meat or lamb

daging sapi: beef

daun: leaf

daun bawang: spring onion (literally 'onion leaf')

daun jeruk purut: kaffir lime leaf

daun pandan: fragrant spicy–sweet leaf with natural green colouring

daun pisang: banana leaf

daun salam: spicy, tangy leaf

delima: pomegranate

dendeng: seasoned and dried (beef)

durian: 'stinky fruit' (very strong-smelling tropical fruit)

E

ebi (kering): dried prawns

emping: crackers made from melinjo nut

es: ice

G

gandaria: plum mango (sour tropical fruit)

garam: salt

godok: boiling, boiled

goreng: frying, fried

gula aren: palm sugar

gula bali: Balinese (palm) sugar

gula jawa: Javanese (palm) sugar

gulai: preparation for curry

H

hijau: green

I

ikan: fish

ikan jambal: fried, salted and dried fish

Ikan teri: dried fish

J

jagung: corn

jahe: ginger

jambu: guava (tropical fruit)

jamur kuping: 'cloud ears' (Chinese mushroom)

jawa: Java

jeruk: citrus

jeruk bali: pomelo

jeruk besar: grapefruit

jeruk manis: orange

jeruk purut: kaffir lime (the leaf in particular is used in cooking)

jinten: cumin

K

kacang: bean pods or fruit (general), including peanuts

kacang goreng: roasted peanuts

kacang hijau: mung beans

kacang kedeleh: soy beans

kacang panjang: snake beans

kaldu: broth

kambing: goat or lamb

kangkung: water spinach (leafy vegetable)

kapulaga: cardamom

kare: curry

kayu manis: cinnamon

kecap: spicy soy sauce

kecap asin: salty soy sauce

kecap ikan: fish sauce

kecap manis: sweet soy sauce

kecap sedeng: sweet–salty soy sauce

kelabat: fenugreek

kelapa, klapper: coconut

kelengkeng: longan (lychee-like tropical fruit)

kemangi: Indonesian basil (lemon basil)

kembang pala: mace

kemiri: candlenut (tropical nut)

kencur: orange galangal or 'bitter root' (ginger-like root)

kentang: potato

kering: dry, dried

ketan: glutinous rice

ketimun: cucumber

ketumbar: coriander seeds

kluwak: Asian truffle (seeds of *Pangium edule*, used as flavouring)

kubis: cabbage

kucai: (garlic) chives

kuning: yellow

kunyit, kunir: turmeric

kuping tikus: 'mouse ears' (Chinese mushroom)

krupuk (udang): prawn crackers

L

labu: pumpkin or melon

laksa: rice noodles or noodle soup

lalap: raw or blanched vegetables

laos, lengkuas: white/pink galangal (ginger-like root)

lapis: layer, layers

lemper: filled rolls of sticky rice

lobak: type of turnip or radish

lombok: large chilli

lontong: long-boiled sticky rice cakes

M

mangga: mango

manggis: mangistan (tropical fruit)

mangkok: cup

manis: sweet

melinjo: bitter nut (used for emping)

merah: red

merica: pepper

mie: wheat noodles

minyak kelapa: coconut oil

N

nanas: pineapple

nangka: 'jackfruit' (type of breadfruit)

nasi: cooked rice

nasi goreng: fried rice

nasi kuning: yellow rice (served at special occasions)

nasi putih: boiled white rice

nasi rames: boiled rice with side dishes

nasi tumpeng: rice mountain shaped into a cone

P

pala: nutmeg

pandan: fragrant spicy–sweet leaf with natural green colouring

panggang: roasting, roasted

pedas: spicy, strong

pepaya: papaya (tropical fruit)

perkedel: fritters or meatballs

petai, peteh: 'stink bean'

petis (udang): black paste made from fermented shrimps

pisang: banana

pisang tanduk: plantain (starchy banana suitable for frying)

putih: white

R

rambutan: 'hairy lychee' (tropical fruit)

rames: mixed, to mix together

rawit: small, very spicy chilli

rebung: bamboo shoots

roti: bread

S

salam: spicy, tangy leaf

sambal: chilli paste (typical Indonesian condiment)

santan: coconut milk

sapi: beef

satay: pieces of roasted meat or fish on skewers

sayur: 'wet' vegetable dish

sayuran: vegetables

sedeng: average, sweet–salty

selada: salad

Selamat makan: Enjoy your food

semur: simmered or stewed

serai: lemongrass

serundeng: spicy grated and fried coconut

sop: thin soup or broth

soto: full, thick soup

susu: milk

sutil: stir-fry spatula

su-un: glass noodles

T

tahu: tofu

tapioca: 'pearls' of dried cassava

tauco: 'bean sauce' (Chinese sauce made from fermented soy beans)

tauge: bean sprouts

telur: egg

tempeh: a textured fermented soybean cake

tepung beras: rice flour

tepung ketan: sticky rice flour

terung: eggplant

tomat: tomato

trassi, trasi or terasi: dried shrimp paste

trassi bakar: roasted dried shrimp paste

tutup: closed or sealed

U

ubi: sweet potato

udang: prawns

udang kering: dried prawns

ulek: grinding

ulekan: pestle

W

wajan: wok (stir-fry pan with round bottom)

Index